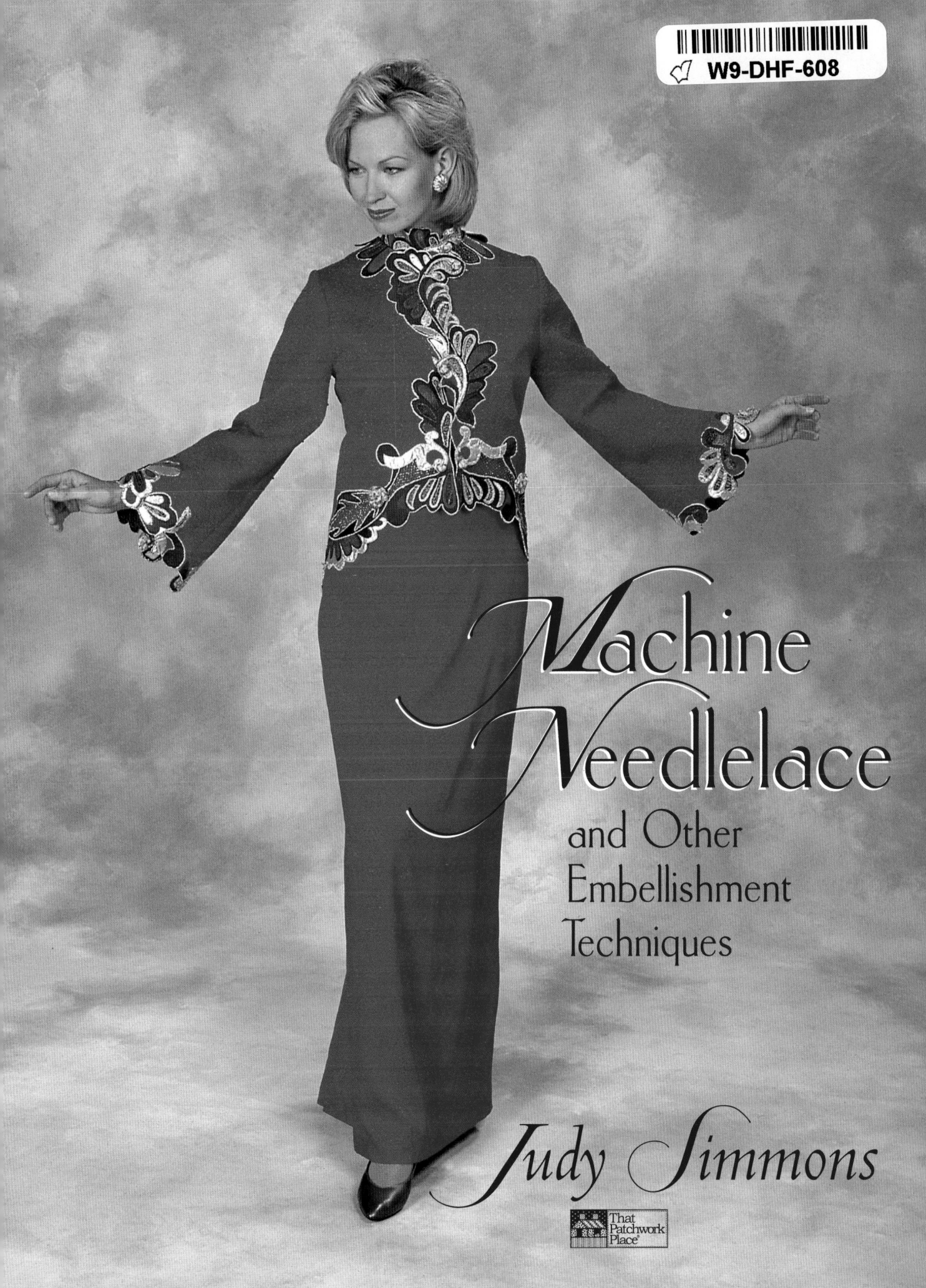

Machine Needlelace

and Other Embellishment Techniques

Judy Simmons

That Patchwork Place®

Dedication

In loving memory of my mother, Alice, whose enthusiasm and love of sewing rubbed off on me.

Acknowledgments

Many people were influential in my development as a fiber artist and in the development of this book. To all of them, I wish to say thank you.

To my mother, Alice, and my grandmother, Ethel, wonderful stitchers who taught me to sew and nurtured my creative growth;

To my children, Jill and Michael, who provide continuing encouragement and think everything I create is great (even when it's not);

And to my husband, John, for all your support. You're the best!

To the talented fiber artists who have contributed to the success of this book: Monica Anderton, Patsy Eckman, Marjorie McDonald, and Susan Vernon. You are truly artists in every sense of the word!

To Julie and Jack Pierce, my wonderful Bernina® dealers and friends. You always come through for me;

To my friends and computer experts, Jeff Garbers and Robin Hollstein, for bailing me out of my computer messes and teaching me how to live with and love my computer;

To my editor, Barabara Weiland, for her incredible help, support, and words of encouragement the past two years;

To all my friends at That Patchwork Place, who have given so much time and understanding to make this a positive experience for me;

To all my students, who have become my dearest friends over the years, for your encouragement and support. I love you all!

Crimson Dynasty

(Shown on previous page) Red and fuchsia hand-painted silk charmeuse highlight this jacket and dress ensemble, which appeared in the prestigious Fairfield Fashion Show. Sleeve, collar, and hemline edges of the jacket feature extensively embroidered appliqués of hand-painted purple silk and gold tissue lamé with intricately worked machine needlelace. The back of the dress, made from sheer, hand-painted red silk chiffon, echoes the appliqué design. Five different red and hot pink metallic couching yarns were used to machine quilt the jacket. Austrian crystals sewn here and there add sparkle. Photo by Frank Riemer.

Credits

Editor-in-Chief . . . . Kerry I. Hoffman
Technical Editor . . . . Barbara Weiland
Managing Editor . . . . Judy Petry
Design Director . . . . Cheryl Stevenson
Text and Cover Designer . . . . Kay Green
Production Assistants . . . . . Marijane E. Figg, Claudia L'Heureux
Copy Editors . . . . Liz McGehee, Melissa Riesland
Illustrator . . . . Brian Metz
Illustration Assistant . . . . Robin Strobel
Photographer . . . . Brent Kane
Models . . . . Melissa A. Lowe, Lisa McKenney

---

MISSION STATEMENT

WE ARE DEDICATED TO PROVIDING QUALITY PRODUCTS AND SERVICE BY WORKING TOGETHER TO INSPIRE CREATIVITY AND TO ENRICH THE LIVES WE TOUCH.

Machine Needlelace and Other Embellishment Techniques
©1997 by Judy Simmons

That Patchwork Place, Inc.
PO Box 118
Bothell, WA 98041-0118 USA

Printed in Hong Kong
02 01 00 99 98   6 5 4 3

Library of Congress Cataloging-in-Publication Data

Simmons, Judy,
    Machine needlelace and other embellishment techniques / Judy Simmons.
        p. cm.
        ISBN 1-56477-162-8
        1. Needlepoint lace. 2. Embroidery, Machine. 3. Machine appliqué. I. Title.
TT805.N43S56 1997
746.2'24—dc21   96-50427
                                                              CIP

Table of Contents

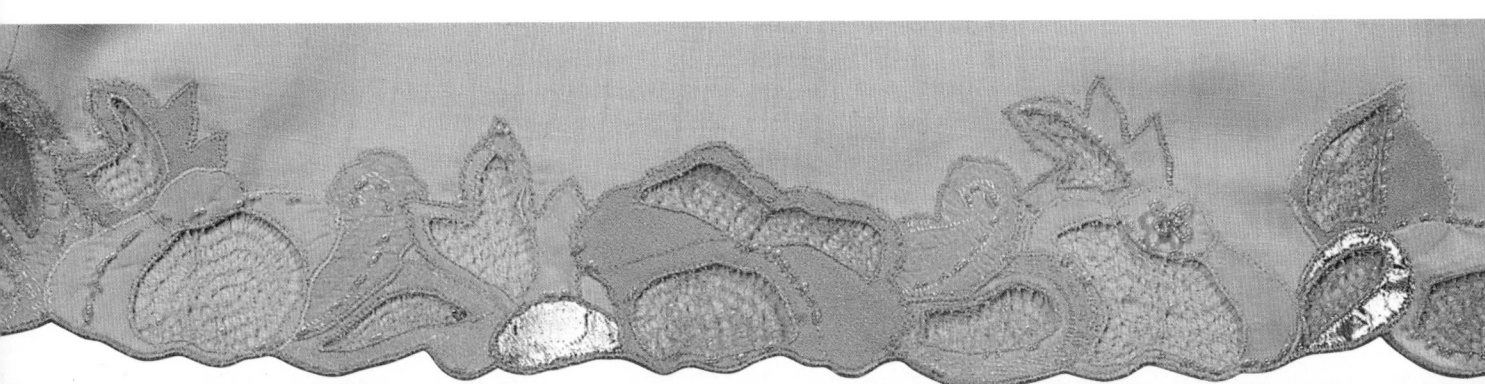

Introduction

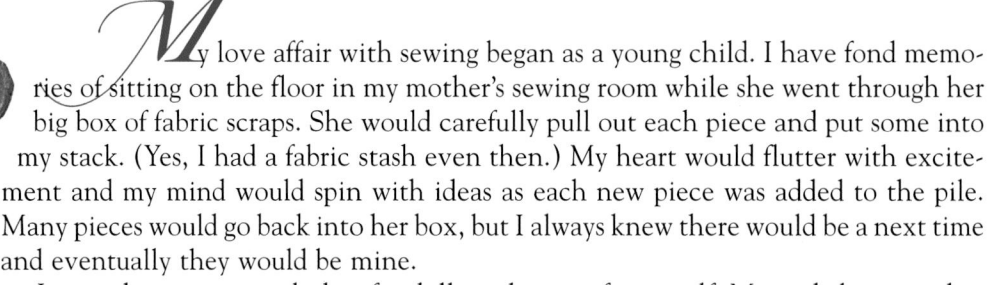

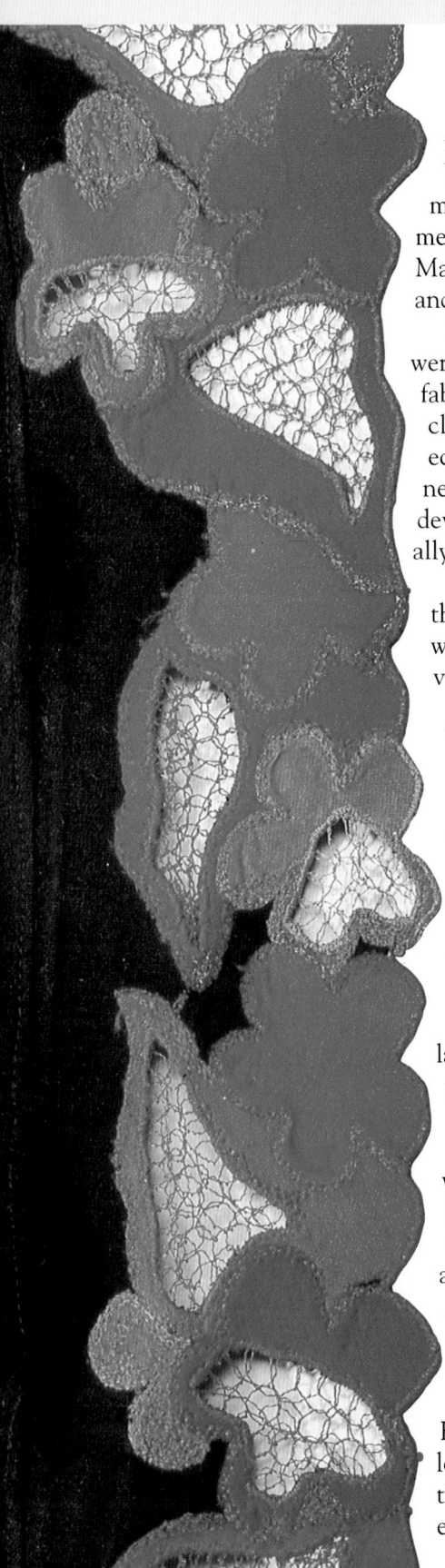

My love affair with sewing began as a young child. I have fond memories of sitting on the floor in my mother's sewing room while she went through her big box of fabric scraps. She would carefully pull out each piece and put some into my stack. (Yes, I had a fabric stash even then.) My heart would flutter with excitement and my mind would spin with ideas as each new piece was added to the pile. Many pieces would go back into her box, but I always knew there would be a next time and eventually they would be mine.

I spent hours sewing clothes for dolls and purses for myself. My inch-long stitches were horrendous, but I thought they were great, and I loved every moment I spent with fabric and thread. I continued to sew throughout my teen years, making my school clothes. My love of sewing led to a degree in home economics. After teaching home economics for many years, I left to raise my children, but the strong desire to create never left me. It found new expression in quilting shops where I taught classes and developed a love for quilts and wearable art. That led to invitations to teach nationally, a real honor for me.

It is because of my teaching and my contact with so many wonderful people that this book has become a reality. Encouragement and requests for a book about my work and the techniques I use to create my wearable art steered me to this new adventure.

In the past few years, I have become involved with creative machine techniques. While living in Florida, I discovered a technique called Richelieu embroidery (or cutwork) in a class I took from Judy Morris, a talented teacher. Traditionally done by hand, this new-to-me cutwork method was done on the machine and added delicate texture to the surface of my fiber art—and it was fun!

Traditional cutwork, dating back to the sixteenth century, requires that holes be cut from the fabric. The holes are then strengthened with a handworked running stitch and anchored with thread bars covered with buttonhole stitches—tedious and time-consuming at best. Small picots, knots, and decorative loops are added for even more dimension. Needle artists found that by building stitches upon each other, they could create "stitches in the air," and the concept of needle-made lace was born. Great noblemen were the first to own and flaunt this popular and painstaking work. For many centuries, it remained a luxury for the rich and a pastime for the leisured class.

Although nothing can replace the beauty and delicacy of handmade needlelace, we have come a long way since then. While contending with more active, high-tech lifestyles, people have turned to their machines to make the modern equivalent of this lace. The results are wonderful to look at and to wear, and are accomplished in a fraction of the time.

Today's machine needlelace is pretty, delicate, and versatile. I've spent endless hours experimenting and creating my own variations of this classic and time-honored art.

Using the many different threads available is both challenging and inspiring. Each one—from lightweight rayons to glittery metallics to heavy couching yarns—lends a different look. Using a natural-fiber thread such as a silk to make lace, and then painting the lace with silk paint produces unique results. Beads and pearls add even more dimension.

One of the other things that makes this work possible is the availability of a variety of stabilizing materials. By supporting the work temporarily, they open the door to even more creativity.

Dimensional needlelace—dragonflies, butterflies, and leaves—are a trademark of mine. Adding wire to the edges makes it possible to manipulate and shape these pieces for a touch of reality. This work adds excitement to wearables and to quilts.

Machine needlelace is appropriate for a variety of clothing styles. I love the delicacy it adds to a neckline, a collar, or the hemline of a skirt. It is also appropriate embellishment for many other types of fiber art, quilts included, and for home-decorating items.

Despite its complex appearance, machine needlelace is surprisingly easy to master and requires minimal precision. All you need is a zigzag sewing machine and the desire to learn. If you're ready to let go of conventional notions about how to use your machine and have a desire to experiment, the avenues of creative expression offered in this book will result in some very creative work of your own. I have tried to include everything you need to know to get started plus a few practice projects to help develop your stitching skill.

My goal in writing this book was to share with you a new approach to the beautiful, time-honored technique of needlelace. Over the years, I have developed a style that reflects the things I love, drawing inspiration from something I've seen in nature or from a subconscious thought stemming from exposure to a piece of art. The creative process enables me to express my passions in fiber. I pass my ideas on to you in the hope that you, too, will be inspired to reach new horizons in your exploration of the sewing machine. Enjoy the journey.

Judy Simmons

Alice's Flower Garden

My mother, Alice, was an avid flower gardener, so I named this garment, the first I made following her death, as a loving tribute to her. To begin, I hand dyed white silk noil to a vibrant shade of red—the perfect backdrop for appliquéd flowers, needlelace, couched strips, and bobbin work. The blouse and jacket lining were made from China silk, hand painted, and then mottled.

$\mathcal{A}$s with any other fiber-art technique, having the right tools and supplies on hand makes learning and exploring more fun and satisfying.

Sewing Machine

A well-maintained sewing machine with a zigzag stitch is adequate for this work. It's important to have a good understanding of your machine. If your dealer does not offer classes, take time to go through the manual, slowly and without interruption if possible. Practice stitches and try out the attachments and presser feet that come with your machine. On occasion, treat yourself to a new presser foot or accessory and learn how to use it.

If your machine is in need of an overhaul, take it to a reputable dealer for servicing and continue to do so on an annual basis. Most owner's manuals provide explicit directions for oiling (if required) and cleaning. Always sew on a fabric scrap for several inches to distribute and remove any excess oil.

Special-Purpose Presser Feet

Check your accessory box for these special-purpose feet to make your projects easier and more successful. The feet for your machine may look slightly different than those shown above right, and they may have slightly different names; check your manual or ask your machine

dealer if they are available for your machine. You may be able to find some common feet through a mail-order supplier. (See "Resources" on page 95.)

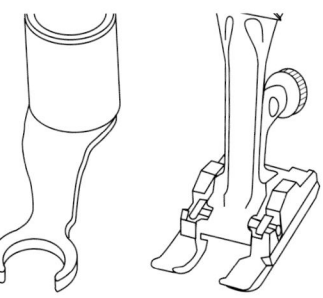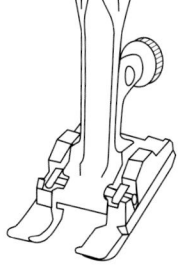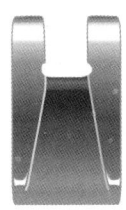

Open-Toe Darning Foot   Machine-Embroidery Foot   Large groove on underside of machine-embroidery foot

The *open-toe darning foot* is not usually included with most machines, but is available for some. It is worth the investment for needlelace as well as for other stitching. It is identical to the darning foot, except that a small section has been eliminated in the front for greater visibility while you work. I consider this foot essential for free-motion work.

The *appliqué or machine-embroidery foot* is standard equipment for most machines. If not, it is well worth purchasing. Also called an open-toe foot, this clear plastic or metal foot allows for a high degree of stitching visibility. A long groove on the underside allows the foot to glide over heavy decorative stitching. It is ideal for satin stitching, which is also used in needlelace.

Needles

Sewing-machine needles play an important role in making needlelace. The wide variety of needles now available makes it easy to do a variety of stitches using special threads without encountering stitch-quality problems. The American numbering system for needle size uses the lower numbers (9, 11, 14, 16, etc.), while the European system uses higher numbers (70, 80, 90, 100, etc.). The lower the number, the finer the needle and the smaller the eye. A size 9/70 needle is good for stitching on sheer and thin fabrics with delicate fibers. Size 14/90 is an average size and works well on most fabrics. The larger needle sizes, 16/100 and above, are designed for heavier fabrics and thicker threads.

The most important concern is that the needle pierces the fabric without damaging the fibers. If the needle is too large, it is likely to break the yarns in the fabric, causing snags and pulls. Since thread passes through the eye several times before actually making the locked stitch, the size of the eye can affect the performance of the thread. The eye must be large enough to prevent the thread from shredding or breaking.

Appliqué and embroidery needles are especially important for decorative machine stitching. They provide a good balance between needle and eye size. Some decorative threads, such as rayon and metallic machine-embroidery threads, break easier than the traditional mercerized cotton-covered polyester threads. A larger-eyed needle is beneficial when using these delicate threads, but many fabrics are too fine for a larger needle. Appliqué and embroidery needles are fine and have a longer eye designed for specialty embroidery threads. The scarf on the back of Metalfil™ needles by Lammertz® and the embroidery needle by Schmetz® are specially designed to eliminate stripping and fraying of specialty embroidery threads. (The scarf is the indentation at the back of the needle that allows the upper and lower threads to lace together in the bobbin area to make a stitch.) Check with your dealer if you are in doubt about which needles work best on your machine.

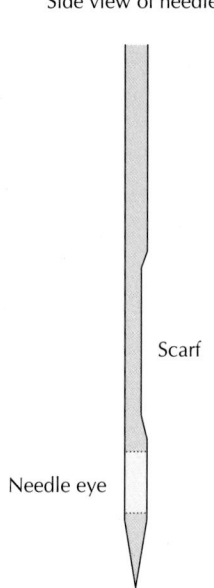

Side view of needle

Scarf

Needle eye

Twin needles, two parallel needles attached to a single shaft, create exciting stitch variations. They are available in different sizes that define the distance between the two needles, and therefore the distance between the two rows of stitching. Twin needles are sold mainly for pintucking with the pintuck foot, but I've found ways to use them to create beautiful needlelace effects. (See "Twin-Needle Stitching" on page 65).

FRESH START

Put a new needle in your machine when you start a project. When you switch to special needles, don't throw out your older but still usable needles. Keep them in a large pincushion marked off by size and needle type (i.e., size 70 embroidery).

Scissors

Scissors and shears in a variety of sizes are essential to the success of any sewing project. I keep mine under lock and key away from anyone who might even think about borrowing them for some purpose other than sewing. I periodically oil them (in the screw area) and have them professionally sharpened. Sharp shears are essential for cutting out the fabric for your garment. Keeping your scissors in a protective plastic cover when not in use is a good idea.

Embroidery scissors are essential for doing the fine cutting and trimming required in appliqué and needlelace. Embroidery scissors should be 3" to 4" in length with sharp points to handle intricate cutting.

Appliqué scissors, although odd looking, are an invaluable tool. The sharp, flattened tips, along with the accentuated curvature of the handle, allow you to get very close to the fabric while trimming pieces of thread and fabric not easily snipped with regular scissors.

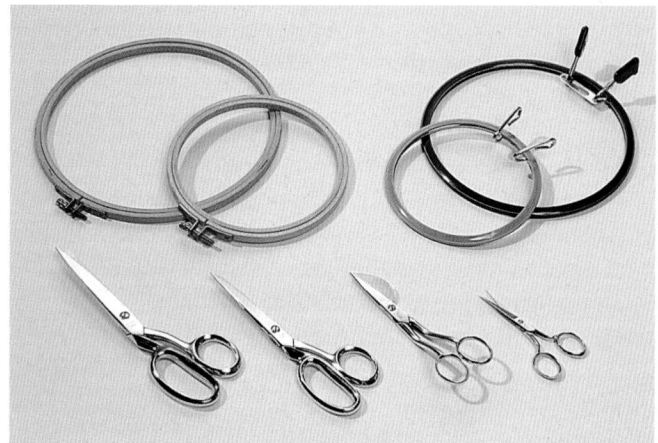

Embroidery Hoops

You will need an embroidery hoop for needlelace and other types of decorative machine stitchery. Some of the available styles are inappropriate for certain types of machine work. For example, wide-rimmed wooden hoops are difficult to get under the presser foot. Special wooden hoops made specifically for machine work have a narrower rim for easier maneuvering. Beveling on the rim provides a smoother, snag-free edge. The hoop has a screw for controlling the tightness of the fabric—especially important when the fabric must be taut.

When using a wooden hoop, wrap the inside rim with narrow twill tape. This holds the fabric more securely and reduces snags in sheer or other delicate fabrics.

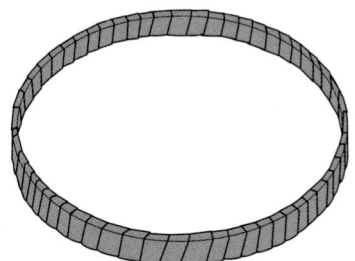

I also use a spring hoop. This very narrow hoop has a bottom ring made of plastic. The top, metal ring has a handle with two arms that you pinch together to fit it securely inside the plastic ring. Releasing the handles tightens the hold on the fabric. This setup gives less control over the tightness of the fabric in the hoop, but allows for a minimum amount of tension on the fibers, vital when working with sheer fabrics. Using the wrong hoop on delicate fabrics can cause the threads to separate. Spring hoops come in several sizes. If you can purchase only one, I recommend a 7"-diameter hoop.

Stabilizers

Stabilizers are special fabrics designed to support machine-embroidery work and to prevent fabric distortion, puckering, tunneling, and skipped stitches. Stabilizers are temporarily pinned or ironed onto the wrong side of the base fabric, under the area to be sewn. The extra layer provides additional stability during stitching. The machine's performance as well as the stitch quality is noticeably different when you use a stabilizer.

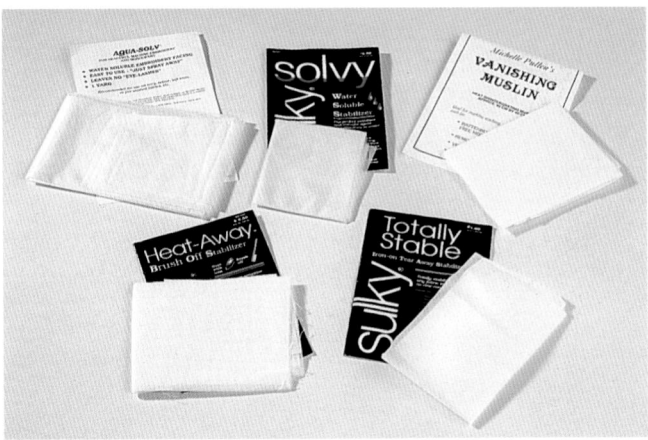

After completing the stitching, the stabilizer is removed by tearing or dissolving it away, or applying heat to disintegrate it. The method depends on the stabilizer you choose. Stabilizers are available in a variety of forms, including paper, woven and nonwoven fabric, and plastic. I recommend keeping a supply of each type on hand. You'll be amazed how often you reach for one to solve a stitching challenge!

Water-soluble stabilizer disintegrates in water and is essential for many types of free-motion work. Fortunately, there are many good ones available. Plastic stabilizer, resembling thin plastic bags, is a popular choice. Place this stabilizer under the area to be stitched, complete the stitching, and then remove it by soaking or misting it with water. Plastic stabilizer dissolves at any water temperature. You can actually tear much of it away, carefully so as not to distort the stitching. Misting may be all that's required to remove the rest.

While I have found that a single layer of plastic stabilizer is adequate for most work, there are times when you may wish to use more than one layer, especially when doing very dense stitching.

Most brands of plastic stabilizer are packaged in precut sheets. Keep the stabilizer sealed in a plastic bag. Air exposure can dry it out, while excess humidity can cause stickiness—maybe even partially dissolving it over time.

In addition to plastic stabilizers, you will also find sheer-fabric stabilizer, such as Melt-A-Way™ by Madeira®. Fabric-like stabilizers are soluble in hot water only; however, they also support heavier forms of machine work—a major benefit. For example, creating lacy filigree stitching and adding machine-embroidered designs or monograms on top are easy with fabriclike stabilizer. Plastic stabilizer eventually rips under dense stitching, but this is not likely to happen with the fabriclike stabilizer.

Heat-disintegrating stabilizer turns to ash under the heat of an iron (as shown in the photo below). You can brush it away; I use a clean toothbrush for this purpose. You can also rub the lace between your hands to loosen the stabilizer. This type of stabilizer works well with all types of fabrics. Even though a high heat is required to disintegrate it, I have used it successfully with heat-sensitive fabrics; the stabilizer acts as a buffer between the iron and fabric. In my experience, the professional quality, steam-intensive irons that some stitchers now own give off a slightly lower heat, which makes them perfect for disintegrating this stabilizer. If in doubt about whether a heat-disintegrating stabilizer is suitable for your thread and fabric combination, test first. These stabilizers are not appropriate when working with the new flat, shiny metallic threads, which are heat sensitive, so opt for a water-soluble stabilizer instead. Store heat-disintegrating stabilizer in a sealed plastic bag away from heat and sunlight.

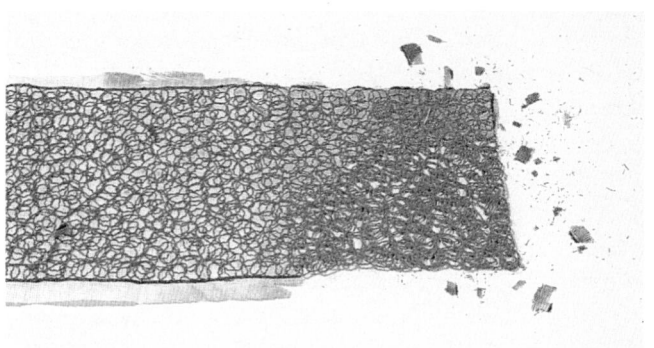

Fusible Web

Fusible web is a layer of nonwoven, heat-sensitive fibers with or without a transfer-paper backing. For the techniques in this book, choose one with paper backing. Ironing on the paper side bonds the exposed web to fabric. Peeling away the paper exposes a side that can be fused to the fashion fabric. This is especially useful when preparing and positioning appliqués for machine stitching. It stabilizes both fabrics so it is easier to sew the appliqué in place with smooth, unrippled edges.

Fusible web is available in a range of weights. Use the lighter-weight web for decorative sewing projects. The heavier weights are not suitable for machine stitching. Also, note that all weights of fusible web will stiffen the appliqué area, making handwork difficult.

Markers

Have a number of different kinds of fabric markers on hand for the techniques discussed in this book.

Colored marking pencils work well on most fabrics. They are good for tracing appliqué designs onto fabric, and most are easily removed.

Water-soluble markers are a good choice but require certain precautions. Heat sets their ink, so do not press over any markings. Water-soluble markers will dissolve water-soluble stabilizer. Do not use them to mark a design directly on this stabilizer.

Permanent black-ink, fine-line markers are required for marking on plastic template materials and water-soluble stabilizers.

Black and colored water-soluble markers (used for overhead projectors) are good for indicating detail lines.

Optional Notions

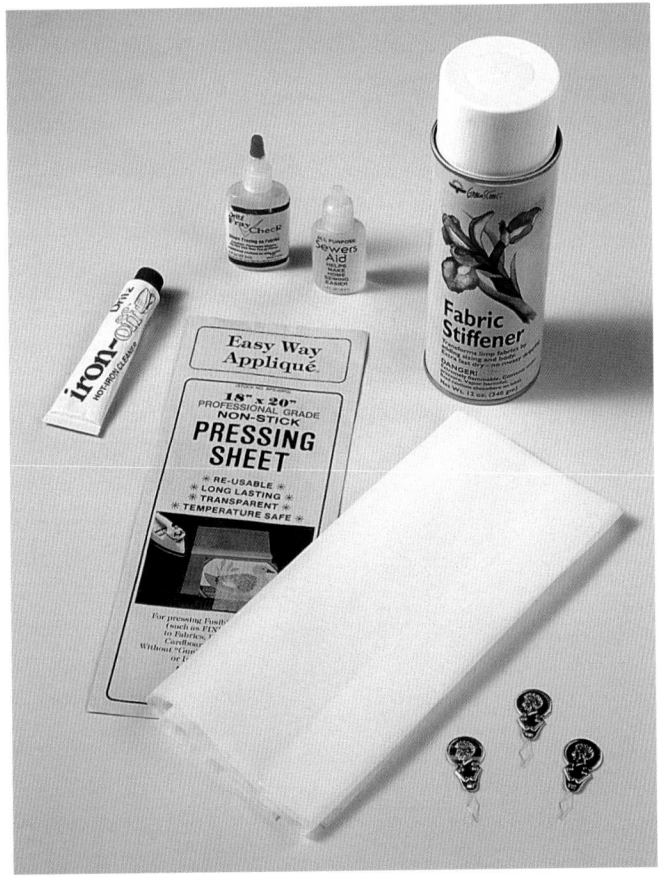

Although the following products (shown above) are not essential, you will find that they often make your work easier.

Liquid silicone, known as Sewers Aid™, helps prevent breaking and shredding of delicate decorative threads. Coat the decorative thread at regular intervals.

Spray-on fabric stiffener is easy to use and gives your fabric the body it needs for creative machine work. It eliminates the need for iron-on stabilizers and washes out easily.

Liquid seam sealant, such as FrayCheck™, is essential for preventing raveling in certain variations of needlelace and when creating lace on heavy fabrics such as velvet and corduroy.

Hot-iron cleaner, such as Iron-off™ by Dritz®, is essential when using fusible web and fusible interfacing. It dissolves virtually all traces of fusible products as well as spray-on starches and stiffeners, which can build up on the sole plate.

A needle threader is helpful with some of the thicker decorative threads. The extra-long threaders sold for sergers work on sewing machines too. Needle threaders tend to break and lose their shape, but are inexpensive.

A Teflon™ pressing sheet is a wonderful addition to your pressing supplies. Use this flexible, plastic-like sheet to protect the iron and ironing board from fusible webs. Use one when working with layered appliqué shapes. Connect the shapes permanently by arranging them on the Teflon sheet as shown in the photo below and then fusing them to each other without fusing them to anything else. This is useful when you want to move the grouping around on the garment before finalizing the design.

Chapter 2

Fabric and Thread

*C*ombining fabric and thread is an exciting part of needlelace and other embellishments. The enormous variety of threads and fabrics available can be intimidating for even the experienced stitcher, so I've suggested thread and fabric combinations to give you an assortment of options. Feel free to experiment with your own combinations.

Over the years, my sewing has taken on a number of distinctive looks, depending on the availability and popularity of certain fabrics. Having worked with a wide variety of fabrics, I always seem to return to natural fibers because they look rich and luxurious. The soft, subtle nature of woolens; the crisp, sharp look of linen; the elegance of silk; and the inviting, comfortable feel of cotton appeal to me more than synthetics and blends. I have had tremendous success with natural fibers, and I use them almost exclusively. However, fabric choice is a reflection of personal taste. Your fabric inventory is influenced by where you live, your budget, and your needs.

◄ *Nature's Palette*

Hand-dyed silk noil creates the backdrop for elaborate appliqué motifs enhanced with rayon and metallic embroidery accents. The appliquéd flowers connect to a Seminole-pieced trellis. Bobbin-couched yarns swirl between motifs for added dimension. The silk charmeuse bodice was machine quilted with rayon and metallic thread, following the lines of the hand-marbled pattern.

Mushroom Medley

Ultra Suede® was the perfect choice for the mushroom stems on this woodlands vest. I ventured away from the sewing machine to hand appliqué the mushroom caps with hand-dyed fabrics. Shaded appliqué on the stems and machine embroidery connect the appliqués for a free-flowing design.

Background Fabric

If machine embellishment is new to you, the most important rule to remember is to choose a fabric that is easy to handle and has enough body to support the decorative work. The techniques discussed throughout this book work best on medium to tightly woven fabrics. Because loosely woven fabrics have more space between the yarns, they are fairly limp and the weave is unstable. Heavy machine work distorts and even damages loose weaves. Knit fabrics can also be difficult to use because of the amount of give in them. If you must use a knit or loosely woven fabric, fuse lightweight tricot knit interfacing to the wrong side to add stability.

Medium-weight fabrics lend themselves beautifully to machine-needlelace and appliqué techniques. Examples include denim, linen and linenlike fabrics, silk broadcloth, silk noil and silk suitings, cotton broadcloth, poplin, faille, gabardine, and tropical-weight wool crepe. Ultra-sheer fabrics, such as organza and synthetic chiffon, are especially beautiful when used with needlelace. Their weave is tight and has enough body to support the lace, especially when sewn with a more delicate thread.

Heavy fabrics such as velveteen, corduroy, and coating-weight wool are good choices for most decorative machine art. Some may require extra measures or adaptations to support needlelace. (See "Pile Fabrics" on page 52.)

As you make your fabric selection, consider a wide range of medium-weight plain-weave fabrics—both smooth and rough surfaced. Consider fabrics made with natural fibers as well as synthetics, and don't disregard blends as potential background fabrics. As you develop skill, consider creating texture with decorative weaves, slubbed yarns, and special threads.

I gravitate toward solid-colored fabrics because they offer a less cluttered work surface. I can visualize all kinds of wonderful things happening on the surface, with the embellishment becoming the dominant factor in the completed garment. However, even patterned fabrics are suitable for a variety of embellishment methods. I have certainly plied my needle on prints, stripes, and plaids.

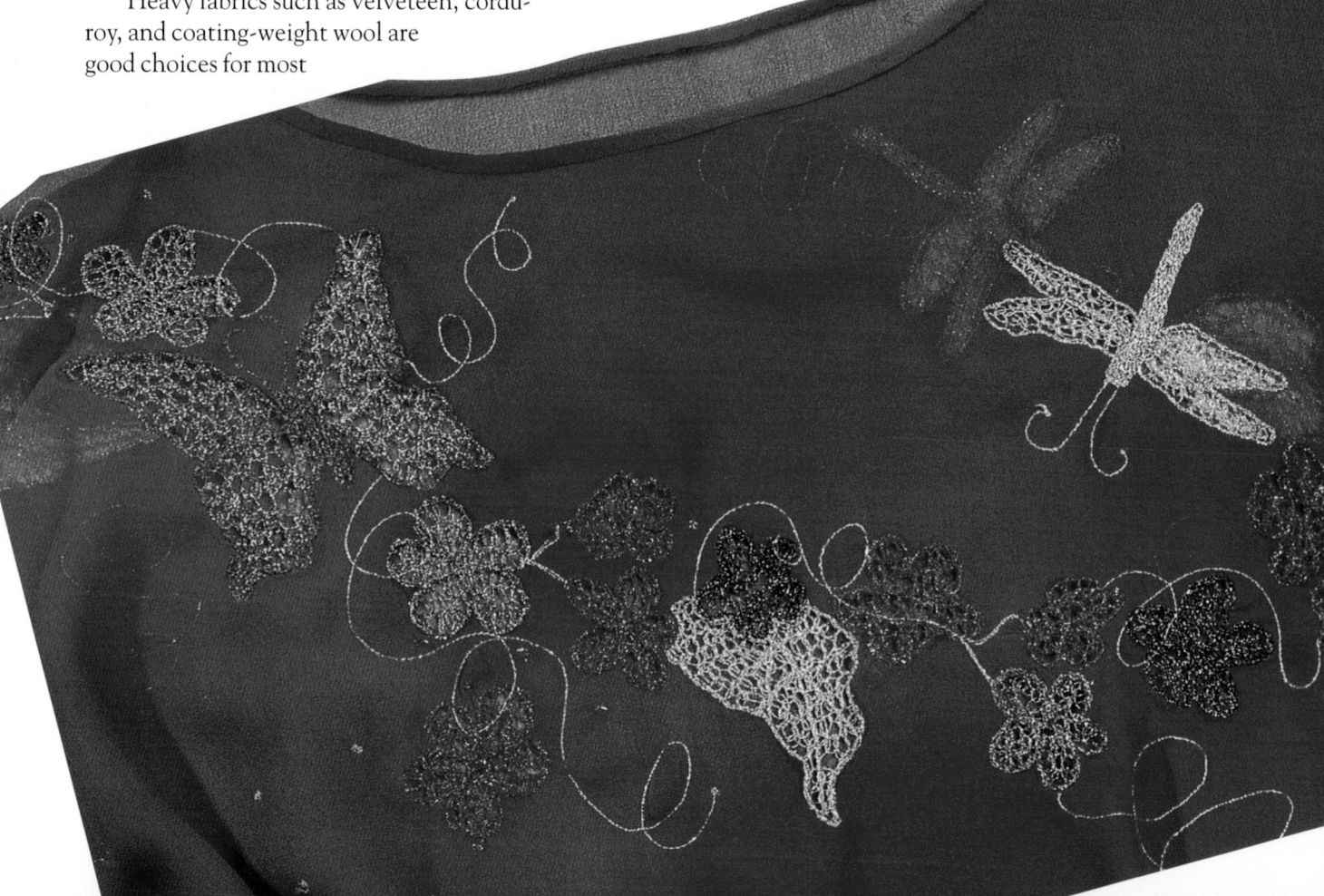

Synthetic suede is a favorite specialty fabric of mine. Although expensive, the rich, luxurious look is like nothing else. This fabric is very receptive to needlelace, as well as many other forms of machine art, because its cut edges don't ravel or fray.

Drapery fabrics with their wonderful bold prints make lovely appliqués as well as borders on clothing. Tapestry fabric is perfect for simple clothing articles embellished with machine embroidery, couching, or needlelace.

Some fabrics require special handling when making needlelace. See pages 52–53 for more information. Directions for making a simple sheer scarf with needlelace are included on pages 53–54 so you can get a feel for handling special fabrics.

Appliqué Fabrics

Most fabrics are appropriate for appliqué as long as they are compatible with your chosen fashion fabric. Choose an appliqué fabric that is the same weight or lighter than the background fabric to eliminate any pulling or distortion.

Make sure your fabrics work together aesthetically. If you have a plain fashion fabric, an appliqué fabric with color movement or texture adds dimension and excitement. Tie-dyed and hand-dyed fabrics, sparkly lamé, and fabrics with a sheen or unusual texture are good choices.

The appliqué and fashion fabrics should have the same flavor when used together. For example, glitzy lamé might look out of place on a wool tweed but perfect on velveteen. For most surface-design techniques, appliqué fabrics are applied with fusible web or stabilized with fusible interfacing. This allows you to choose appliqué fabrics you might not otherwise consider.

Create interesting appliqué fabric using a natural-fiber fabric and silk paint. Natural fibers take dyes and paints well because they are porous and absorb dye with greater intensity. To make shaded appliqué fabrics, see pages 16–17.

MAKING SHADED APPLIQUÉ FABRICS

Much of my work features fabric I create myself using Procion® dyes. I call this "shaded appliqué fabric" because it is strictly that. I do not use it as whole-cloth pieces for clothing or quilts. Instead, I create it with one purpose in mind: to cut it up so variations of shading and colors within the fabric add dimension, movement, and excitement to the appliqué pieces.

Dyeing your own fabric is messy but fun. You can do it in your basement or backyard. Although I now use a process that involves fiber-reactive dyes, and that requires curing the fabric, you can produce a good facsimile with silk paint and muslin. This alternative is particularly good for beginners.

I suggest Deka® silk paint because it is easy to use. It is available at art-supply and crafts stores, or you can order it from one of the mail-order sources listed on page 95.

Consider the following points to create the desired colors.

❧ For the most intense color, use silk paints full strength, straight from the bottle.

❧ To obtain lighter, less-intense colors, add water to silk paint. The more water you add, the lighter the color gets. This is the only way to make tints or pastels, since there is no white paint available.

❧ When mixing paints, use the same brand for the best, most reliable results.

❧ Create a shade of the original color by adding black.

While silk paints work especially well on silk, I recommend muslin for beginners. Some silk paints also work on synthetics. Check the label for fiber compatibility.

Materials

¼ yd. to ½ yd. pieces of bleached
or unbleached high-quality muslin

Silk paint in 3 to 4 colors of your choice

Bucket of water

Plastic-covered work surface

1"- to 1½"-wide inexpensive
paintbrush for each color

Small containers (clean baby-food jars or
clean pet-food tins) for each color

Rubber gloves and apron

Directions

1. Wash the muslin to remove sizing and oil from your hands. The fabric must be thoroughly wet to be a good canvas for the paint. Either paint the wet fabric immediately, or dry and store it until ready to paint. Then, soak the dry fabric in a bucket of water for 10 minutes so the water permeates the fibers.
2. Choose 3 or 4 coordinating colors, such as the warm colors (red, orange, and yellow) or the cool colors (blue, green, and purple). Decide whether you want to use the paints full strength, thinned, or darkened, and prepare accordingly. Pour a small amount of each color into a small jar or tin.

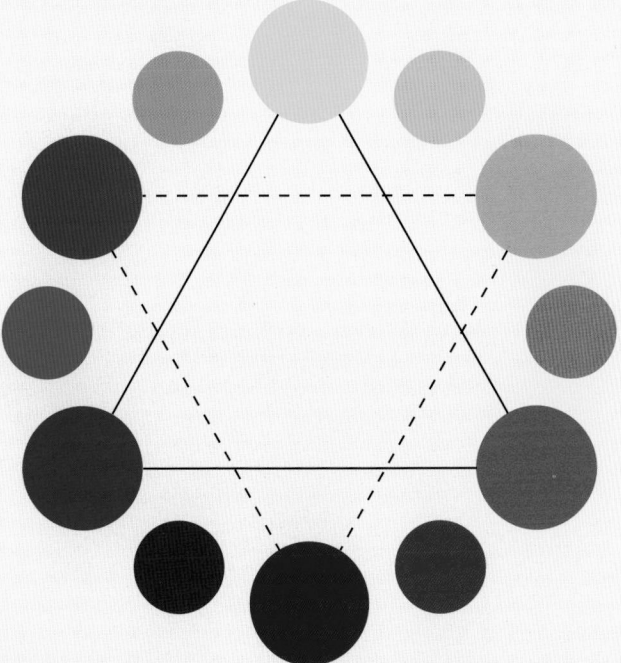

3. Wring the fabric, squeezing out as much water as possible. Spread the fabric on the plastic-covered surface.
4. Dip a clean brush into one of the colors and brush a 3"-diameter (approximate) circle onto the fabric. Repeat every 10" or so, brushing the color randomly.

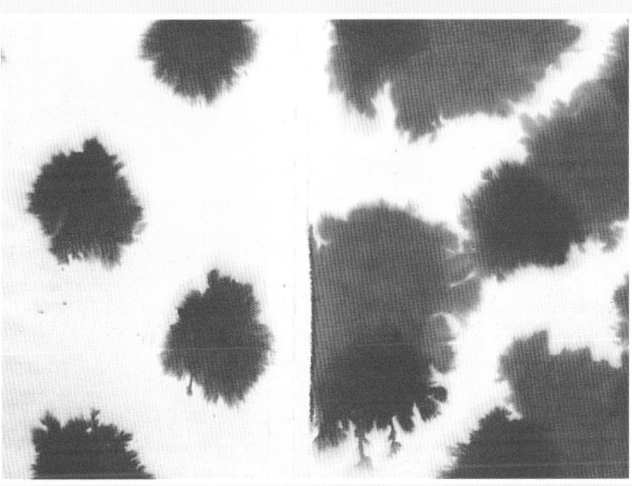

5. With a clean brush, add the second color, positioning it so it touches the first color. Use another brush or your gloved fingers to blend the two colors.
6. Repeat steps 4 and 5 with the third and then the fourth colors.

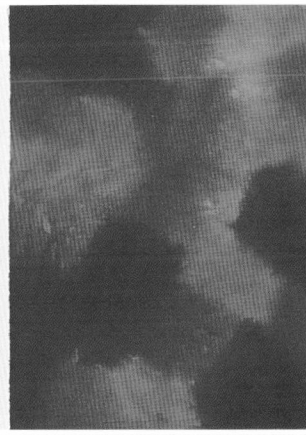

7. Allow the painted fabric to dry completely before proceeding to the next step.
8. Following the paint manufacturer's directions, set the color. Different brands require different methods, some more involved than others. A few don't require setting at all.
9. Rinse the painted fabric in a sink of cool water.

Interfacing

If your garment requires extensive decorative machine work, consider backing the fashion fabric with a lightweight fusible interfacing. This is particularly true for bodices and jackets. Of course, you may not want to interface sheer fabrics, since interfacing changes its character and color.

Interfacing used as a backing does not replace the interfacing you would normally use in areas requiring support, such as necklines, collars, and cuffs, but rather adds stability to the overall shape. The finished garment will also hang better and support the added weight of the embellishment.

I prefer lightweight nylon-tricot knit and woven fusible interfacing. Test two or more interfacings on fabric scraps, stitching through the stabilized scrap, to help you choose your favorite.

Be sure to preshrink the interfacing. For woven and knit interfacings, this means soaking in hot water without agitation until the water is cool. Then, allow the interfacing to dry flat (not in a dryer). Cut the required pieces, using the garment pattern, and fuse them to the wrong side of the corresponding garment pieces, following the manufacturer's directions.

Decorative-Thread Basics

Decorative thread is the key component for lace making and other creative machine work. Today your choices continue to expand; every month seems to bring another new thread or yarn to the local fabric shop. Some threads require special needles or handling for the best results and trouble-free stitching. This section will acquaint you with some of the threads available and offer some special handling advice.

It is important to remember a few basic facts when working with decorative threads.

❧ Most threads are numbered according to thickness. The higher the number, the finer the thread. Fine fabrics usually require finer threads, while heavier fabrics can support the weight of heavier threads.

❧ Though usually not as strong as standard sewing thread, decorative machine threads perform very well with a little coaxing. Use a specialty needle to ensure gentler, shred-free stitching. See "Needles" on pages 7–8.

❧ To reduce stress on the thread, lower the upper tension on your sewing machine by one number. Also try drizzling liquid silicone along the length of the spool to make the thread more manageable.

❧ Blend thread types to achieve unique looks not possible with a single thread. (Thread two threads through a single needle. Do consider garment care when blending threads to make sure all fibers are compatible.) You may need to use a larger needle when blending threads. Test to make sure the needle doesn't damage the background fabric.

❧ Finally (and most important), loosen up and have fun as you try out these special threads and yarns! I do "knuckle checks" in class. This is meant as a joke, but white knuckles alert me to tense students. That tension ultimately shows up in their work as well as in sewing-machine and thread performance.

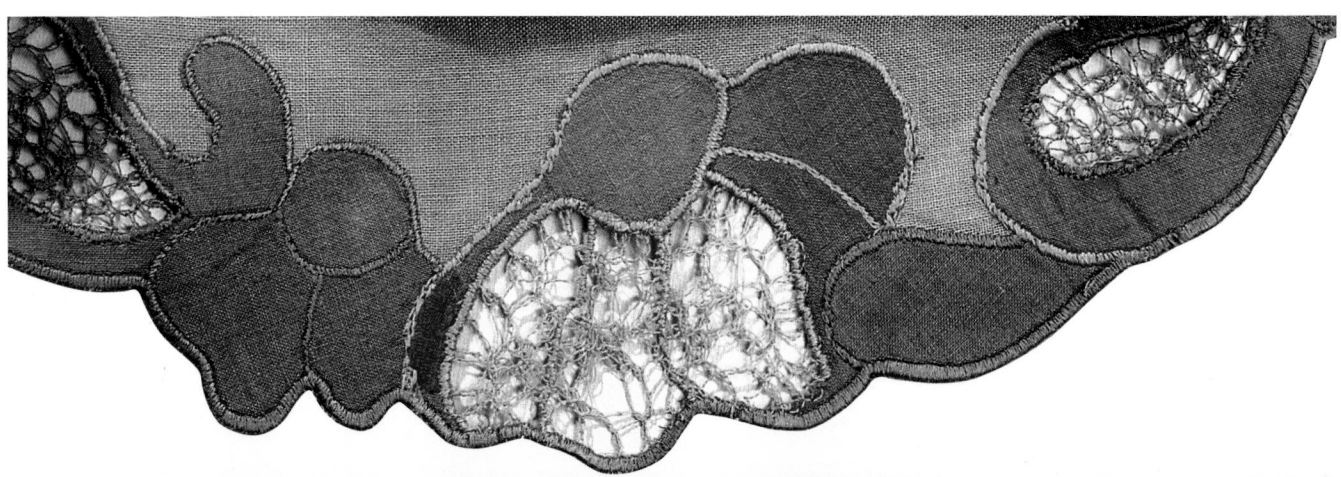

Machine-Embroidery Threads

Rayon machine-embroidery thread is a popular choice for machine art. Even though it is not as strong as standard sewing thread, it has a beautiful luster that adds a bit of sheen to the finished piece. Rayon thread comes in several weights, but #40 is the most common. Some brands have a heavier #30 weight, which is more luxurious and worth trying.

Rayon thread is not twisted as tightly as standard thread, making it seem thicker. This "thickness" adds texture and dimension to the surface of your work. Many rayon threads, such as Natesh®, Sulky®, Madeira®, Mez Alcazar®, and Coats & Clark®, come in a wide range of colors with varying characteristics, including variegated colors. Some brands seem to work into the fabric more evenly, some are stronger and easier to use, and some are available in a wider color range. Experience and experimentation will reveal your personal favorites. However, I have always chosen thread for its color; an exciting color palette contains many brands and types.

Cotton machine-embroidery thread is usually available in a #30- to #80-weight range. It is strong, easy to use, and comes in a wide range of colors, including variegated, except for the 80 weight, which has a more limited selection. Unlike rayon, cotton thread lacks sheen, resulting in a more subtle look.

When choosing a fabric/thread combination, make sure they complement rather than compete with each other. For example, fine linen looks elegant worked in cotton embroidery thread, which is low-key and enhances the linen fiber without detracting from its beauty.

Metallic thread is exciting to use because it adds sparkle to your work. The limited color range is adequate, and since I use metallics with other threads, I can always find one that blends. With its tendency to break, metallic thread can be among the more difficult to use. Use a specialty needle, such as Schmetz® embroidery, Metalfil® by Lammertz®, or a machine-needle size 14/90 or larger to reduce breakage. Use liquid silicone (page 11) with *twisted* metallic threads.

In addition to twisted metallic threads, you will enjoy using flat metallic threads. Stream Lamé Tinsel and Sliver™ resemble old-fashioned Christmas-tree tinsel and are both challenging and rewarding to use. Because these threads are flat, their reflective abilities exceed other metallic threads. They work best with a size 14/90 (or larger) needle on a vertical-spool pin. They are less heat tolerant than other threads, so use them with water-soluble stabilizers when making needlelace.

Flat metallic threads tend to curl as they come off the spool, making threading the needle a challenge. Securely seat the thread between the tension discs to flatten and straighten the thread. Then, use long serger tweezers to thread the needle. Do not use liquid silicone on flat metallic thread as it does not absorb the liquid.

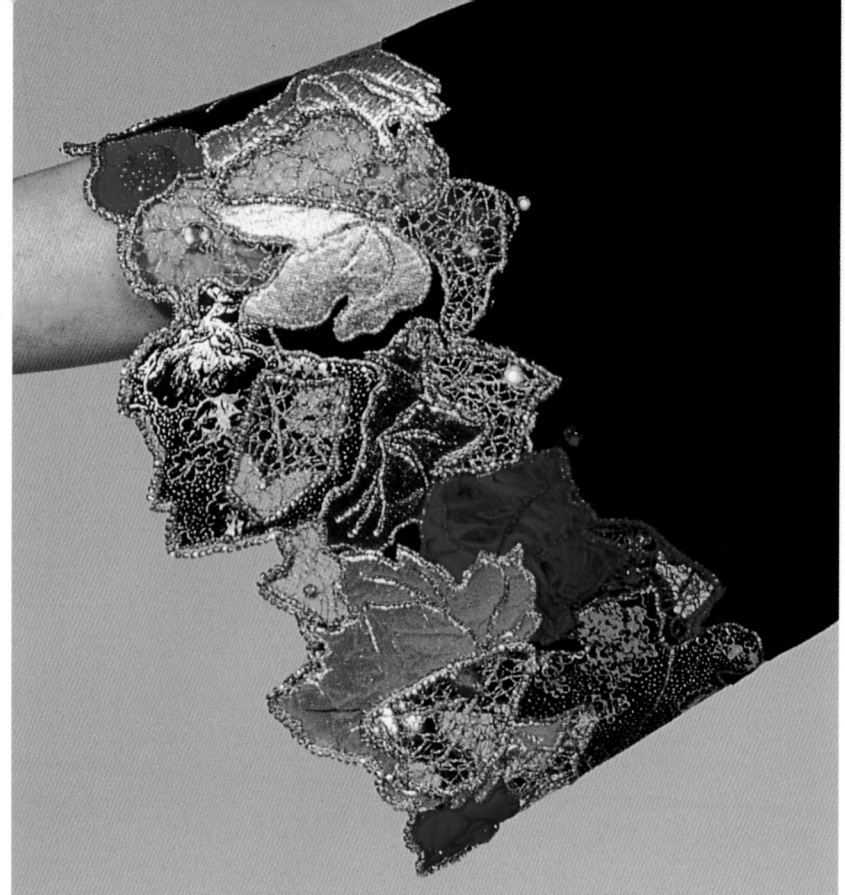

Specialty Threads

Silk thread, a luxurious fiber that guarantees beautiful results, is available in several weights. The #100-weight thread is extremely fine and works well in small areas on delicate or sheer fabrics, such as China silk and organza. The #50-weight, also a fine thread, adds a delicate look to light- and medium-weight fabrics, such as silk broadcloth, charmeuse, and crepe de Chine. The #30-weight, because it is heavier, is more prominent on the surface, giving a richer look.

Variegated threads change color three to four times along a short length of thread.

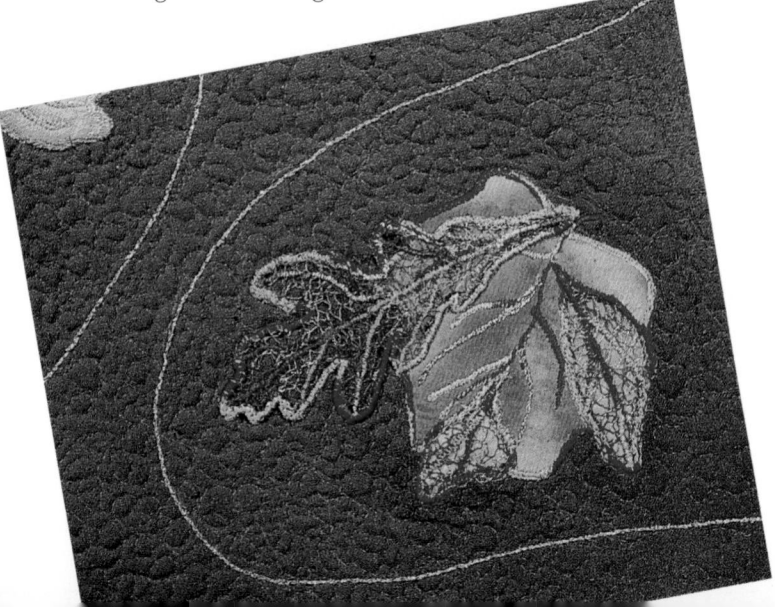

They are great fun to use because of their wonderful color movement. They are widely available in rayon and cotton and in a limited range of metallic colors.

Burmilana is a *wool and acrylic thread* made by Madeira. Its fuzzy texture resembles crewel embroidery yarn. When Burmilana is used to make needlelace on wool or wool-like fabric, the combination is stunning. Use a size 16/100 needle when sewing with this thread. Lint builds up quickly, so clean your machine often.

Nylon or polyester monofilament thread is available in clear and smoke color. This somewhat wiry thread seems to have a mind of its own, but is effective when used in the bobbin. In needlelace, which is open and airy, both top and bottom threads are obvious. A clear bobbin thread doesn't compete with the top thread. In addition, transparent thread adds body to needlelace along necklines, hems, and sleeve edges—areas that require extra support.

Special bobbin threads are finer than other sewing threads. Neutral in color, these threads are usually polyester or cotton-covered polyester. Because they are finer, they eliminate the bulky buildup on the wrong side of the fabric, resulting in smoother machine stitching on the right side.

THREAD TIPS

- The higher the number, the finer the thread. Finer threads produce a finer look.
- Choose thread that is compatible with the weight of the background fabric. Fine threads may get lost in heavily textured fabrics.
- Mix threads for unusual texture and color combinations. Consider the care of the finished piece when combining threads.
- Always use a good-quality thread. The finished product is only as good as the materials that go into it.
- Start collecting thread today to create your stitching palette. I have more than eight hundred spools and I use every one!

Many decorative threads unwind by themselves and there is no way to secure them. You can make plastic thread protectors to hold the thread in place on the spool. Buy very thin clear-vinyl tablecloth material at your fabric store. (You can make more than 100 thread protectors from just 1 yard.) Using a rotary cutter, cut 6"-long strips the height of your spools and mark one end with an adhesive-backed colored dot. Wrap the vinyl strip around the spool, beginning at the *unmarked* end. (The dot makes it easy to locate the end of the strip when you are ready to use the spool.) The vinyl will stick to itself.

Key

1	Novelty threads	5	Radiance	9	Candlelight® metallic yarn	13 Transparent thread
2	Rayon	6	Lurana	10	Braid	14 Variegated cotton
3	Burmilana	7	Sliver	11	Pearl Crown Rayon	15 Silk
4	Metallic	8	Gold	12	Variegated Rayon	16 Ribbon Floss® braided ribbon

THREAD CHARTS

It is helpful to make thread charts for a variety of threads and yarns. When I want to see how a particular thread looks on the surface of a fabric, a quick glance at the chart tells me all I need to know.

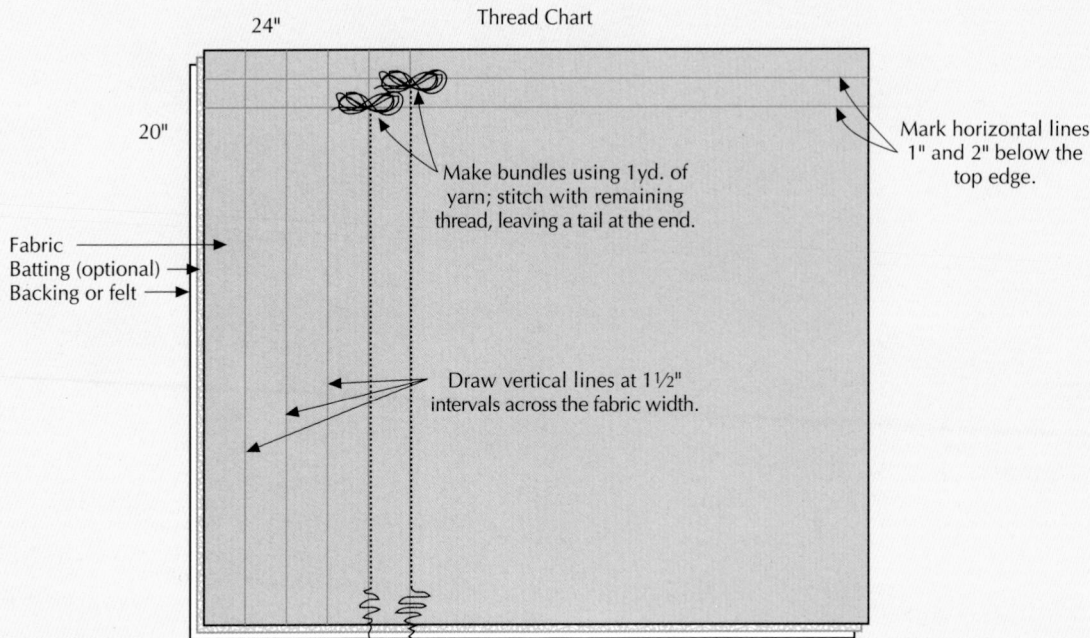

Thread Chart

24"

20"

Make bundles using 1yd. of yarn; stitch with remaining thread, leaving a tail at the end.

Mark horizontal lines 1" and 2" below the top edge.

Fabric
Batting (optional)
Backing or felt

Draw vertical lines at 1½" intervals across the fabric width.

Grouping threads by the same or similar fiber content, such as rayon, metallic, or silk, is one option. Another way is to group the different kinds of one color, or divide threads that can be used in the top spool and those that can only be used in the bobbin.

When making a thread chart, stitch enough to see how the thread looks on the fabric. I also find it helpful to have a fluff of thread at the top so I can see what the thread looks like coming off the spool.

Materials

20" x 24" piece of medium to tightly woven fabric, such as muslin, silk noil, or any linenlike fabric, in a light neutral color

20" x 24" piece of felt and 20" x 24" piece of fusible web for backing

OR

20" x 24" piece of low-loft batting and 20" x 24" piece of backing

Fabric marking pen and fine-point marking pen

2 yds. of each thread or yarn

Transparent monofilament thread for the top spool

Standard sewing thread or special bobbin thread for the bobbin

Directions

Note

The following method creates a thread chart by couching thread to the fabric surface. This method is particularly appropriate for thicker threads and yarns that cannot be fed through the needle. You can also make a thread chart with threads that do feed through the needle. For directions, see "Thread Chart Variation" on page 23.

1. Use the fabric marker to draw horizontal lines 1" and 2" below and parallel to the top edge of the neutral fabric piece.
2. Draw vertical lines parallel to each other and 1½" apart across the fabric width.
3. Fuse the marked fabric to the felt with fusible web, or sandwich it with the batting and backing as shown in the illustration above and pin securely to keep the

layers from shifting while you stitch. (Use small safety pins to avoid pin pricks and scratches as you work.)

4. Thread your machine with monofilament thread on top, and use a special bobbin thread (page 20) or standard sewing thread in the bobbin. Use a regular presser foot, or try a cording foot, which will guide the yarns more easily. Make sure the feed dogs are up and engaged. Set the stitch length to 8 to 10 stitches per inch, and set the stitch width at 2 (or wide enough to encase the yarn as you couch it in place).

5. Working with a 2-yard length of thread or yarn, wind 1 yard of it around a 2"-wide piece of cardboard as if you were making a pompon. Remove the thread bundle and twist once in the center to make a figure eight. Place the bundle at the first horizontal line (1" from the top edge) on the fabric and along one of the vertical lines.

6. Machine stitch through the center of the bundle, and couch the remaining thread along the marked vertical line. To couch, zigzag stitch over the thread, holding it in place on top of the fabric. Stop 2" from the bottom of the fabric and tie off, leaving a 2"- to 3"-long tail of the thread or yarn. (Leaving a tail allows you to compare the thread itself with the thread couched in place.)

7. Couch the second thread in the same manner, placing the thread bundle at the second horizontal line (2" from the top edge). Continue couching threads, alternating the bundle placement in this seesaw manner for better visibility.

8. Using a fine-point marking pen, label each row with the thread brand, fiber content, and any other pertinent information.

9. Finish the raw edges of your thread chart, using a serger or a zigzag stitch. If you wish, add a fabric sleeve on the back or tabs along the top so you can hang the sampler near your machine for easy reference.

Thread Chart Variation

If the decorative threads you are sampling fit through the sewing-machine needle:

1. Set up the machine for a straight stitch of medium length, and replace the transparent thread in the needle with the appropriate decorative thread.

2. Prepare the fabric layers as described in steps 1–3 of "Thread Charts."

3. Stitch on the vertical line, through the fabric layers, with the selected thread. Make a separate thread bundle for each row and sew it in place above the corresponding row of stitching.

Couching Threads

Many heavier threads and yarns cannot be threaded through the top spool, but must be wound onto the bobbin instead. Bobbin couching is done with the fabric right side down. As you sew, the bobbin thread appears on the right side of the fabric.

Bobbin couching is ideal when a heavier look is desired. There are exciting metallic couching yarns available to the fiber artist, including Candlelight® by Y. L. I. and Glamour by Madeira. Kreinik has a wonderful line of specialty threads, including braids, ribbons, cables, and metallics, in a wide range of colors. All these add glimmer and glitz, as well as create dimension and visual interest.

Pearl cotton and rayon threads are particularly effective for bobbin couching. Pearl Crown Rayon lends a subtle sheen to the overall look. Pearl cotton, which comes in several thread weights (#3, #5, and #8), is more refined.

Ribbon Floss is a flat, narrow rayon ribbon and a wonderful addition to your collection. Although too wide for machine lace, it brings radiance to other areas of surface design. You cannot thread it through the needle, but you can use it in the bobbin.

Chapter 3

Designing Your Project

Sheer Magic

Gold metallic leaves float across the surface of this sheer silk organza blouse. Gold filigree buttons repeat the look of the needlelace, which requires special handling when worked on sheer fabrics like this one. A coordinating camisole and skirt of silk crepe de Chine complete the simple but elegant outfit.

*D*esigning wearable art can be the most difficult part of any project, but it can also be fun and rewarding when approached one step at a time.

If designing is new to you, it's important to work within your comfort zone. Striving to achieve a complex work of art the first time out can be overwhelming and discouraging to a beginner. It's far better to start with a simple design and enjoy the process of creating a truly wearable, one-of-a-kind garment.

Selecting a Pattern

Certain garments are more appropriate for decorative machine work. Choosing just the right one can be a challenge. "Keep it simple" is a good rule to live by. Look for designs with simple lines that require minimal seaming and no darts if possible. (Full-figure patterns often include darts or tucks for more shaping over body curves. These can present some design and construction challenges.)

Large areas of uninterrupted space allow you to express your creative energy and ideas. Check out the "easy to sew" sections in pattern books. Independent pattern companies often offer designs specifically shaped for embellishment. Consider these since they often have few seams or darts to interfere with the design work.

I recommend a simple vest pattern for your first project. Perfect for formal to very casual occasions, vests have become a staple in our wardrobes. Their clean, usually dartless shape is the perfect backdrop for embellishment. Other options include:

- ❧ Simple, loosely fitted jackets with minimal seaming and darts and straight sleeves.
- ❧ Set-in sleeves. These hang especially well when decorative machine art is used at the hem edge.
- ❧ Plain necklines and simple collars. They "sing" when dressed in needlelace.
- ❧ Skirts and dresses with limited fullness and simple lines.
- ❧ Hemlines, necklines, and pocket and sleeve edges—perfect places for embellishment.
- ❧ Wrap skirts with a front opening. Try needlelace along the front edge.

Once you find an acceptable pattern, check the fabric recommendations. Choose a fabric that works well for the garment *and* the surface-design technique you are using. Most of the styles described above require a medium-weight fabric, which is also ideal for supporting decorative machine work.

After you are comfortable working on simple patterns, you can move on to more involved designs. Many designer patterns have beautiful lines that are the result of unique construction techniques. This makes them difficult (but not impossible) candidates for surface embellishment. A well-designed garment balances embellishment and construction detail; both should enhance rather than compete with each other. More complex pattern designs require more careful planning. When in doubt, err on the side of less rather than more embellishment.

A designer pattern with seventeen pattern pieces was used to make the red silk noil jacket shown here. The patch pocket includes a double-welt opening. Integrating design elements that cross over seam lines, flow in and out of pockets, around cuffs, and in and around intricate construction features is challenging and fun—and within the reach of the seamstress looking for design and sewing challenges.

Planning a Design

After selecting a pattern, get down to the fun of planning the actual design. Inspiration is everywhere, but you must train your eye to see it. I carry a small notepad so I can jot down ideas that come to me during the day—often from unexpected sources and at unexpected times.

Even if you do not consider yourself an artist, you can rely on simple everyday items in your home for an abundance of design ideas—if you are willing to look at them with fresh eyes. I have used all of the following sources at one time or another for inspiration.

- Consider tracing the shapes of small frames, odd-shaped plaques, cookie cutters, seashells, and stencils. Children's puzzles make wonderful designs. The base outlines of figurines and odd-shaped jewelry provide interesting patterns too.

- Browsing through stores can open your eyes to many possibilities—another great excuse for shopping. Art- and crafts-supply stores abound with shapes perfect for tracing. Check out the wood department for cutouts designed for hand-painting projects. They're often just the right size for appliqués. The elegant French curve found in drafting departments and fabric stores can be used to create any number of new shapes. Hardware stores offer interesting tools, bits of hardware, and small building materials. Collect greeting cards for design inspiration, taking care to adapt and change them to reflect your own creativity and to avoid infringing on someone's copyright.

- Check out remnant and flat-fold tables in your fabric store. You can often simplify the bold design shapes found in home-decorating fabrics. If you trace the shapes onto a sheet of transparent plastic, you can enlarge them using an overhead projector. Or, take your tracing to a photocopy shop to enlarge or reduce it to the desired size. Look carefully at printed fabrics for shapes you can cut out for appliqué.

- Nature provides an abundance of inspiration. Use natural materials, such as leaves and flower petals, to make patterns for appliqué. That's what I used to make the leaf pattern for the velveteen vest that is shown on page 51.

- Books are also a wonderful idea source. Stained-glass designs have beautiful shapes and simple lines; they're ideal for machine art. The specialized coloring books sold in art stores have wonderful line drawings suitable for appliqué and needlelace. Many of these contain copyright-free designs you can trace, then enlarge or reduce at the copy shop. Keep a master copy of the design, noting the percentage it was reduced or enlarged so you can use it for later reference. You'll find lots of simple shapes in children's coloring books. They are an ideal starting point for the beginner.

Once you've chosen a design, make sure it's the appropriate size and scale. Consider its location on the garment and the embellishment techniques you plan to use to execute it. Several design shapes are provided at the back of this book and are appropriately sized and scaled. Compare what you have designed to these shapes and adjust as needed. Rely on your eye too. You are probably more aware of scale and proportion than you realize. If something looks too large or too small to you, it probably is. Learning to trust your instincts is part of the creative process.

Stylizing the Design

After settling on the shape (or shapes) for your design, adapt or stylize it to suit your needs. Some designs are quite intricate, with too many points and curves to successfully execute in any form of machine art. Stylizing simplifies the design for reproduction in fabric and decorative thread.

To stylize a design:

1. Use a marker and trace the design onto tracing paper, simplifying angles, softening points, and eliminating detail lines too intricate to reproduce.

2. Make many copies of the design, including a reverse or mirror image. Having a number of copies to play with speeds up the design process; having mirror images gives you more placement options.
3. Don't be afraid to move lines, add shapes, and adjust the design to fit your needs and the garment shape.

The next step is positioning the design motifs in a pleasing arrangement on your garment pattern. There are many ways to approach this. I work with full-size pattern pieces made from plain newsprint.

To make a duplicate pattern:

1. Pin the original pattern pieces to the newsprint. Cut out the shapes as if you were cutting them from fabric. It is not necessary to transfer any pattern markings to the newsprint. Cut *all* pattern pieces you may want to embellish, making sure to cut a left and right front, left and right back (if there is a center back seam), and a left and right sleeve. If the back is cut on the fold, be sure to cut a complete back from the newsprint.
2. Overlap and pin the fronts and back together along the side seam lines. (You may have to adjust shaped side seams by straightening them so they will lie flat.) Pin the pattern to a design wall so you can view the piece at eye level. Set aside the sleeves for now.

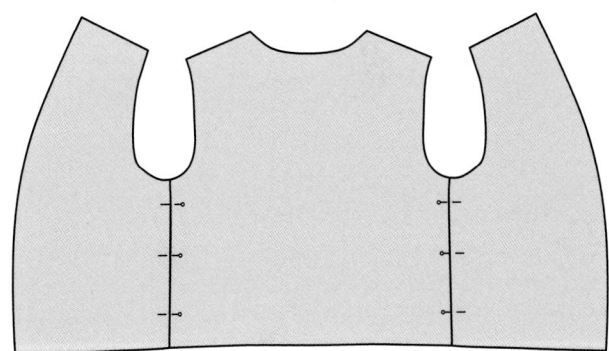

DESIGNING WITH EASE

Try to design a piece at the same angle as it will appear in its finished form. If you don't have a design wall, invest in a 2-yard piece of white or black felt that you can pin up and take down at will. Felt is the perfect backdrop for a paper pattern.

DESIGN AESTHETICS

Before you finalize your design, consider the following basic rules
for creating aesthetically pleasing garment designs.

- Less is more. Fewer elements and a simpler design are almost always better. Do not overdo!
- Integrate the design with the existing seam lines and details. It's OK to arrange elements on top of seam lines. However, seams that are crossed with a design must be permanently stitched before embellishment begins. If designs don't cross seam lines, position them well out of the way of seam allowances so they won't interfere with the construction process.

- When designing two of something, such as a pair of sleeves or pockets, do each one separately. It's more interesting if they are *not* identical, even though the same motifs are used on both. Of course, you may use mirror-image designs if you prefer a more balanced, symmetrical look.
- Don't overlook other design elements when planning motif placement. Stitching with decorative thread can pull appliqués together without overpowering them. Decorative trim or interesting closures are important considerations too. Examine the photos below to see how important it is to make sure the different elements complement rather than compete with each other. Notice how the filigree buttons complement the lace in the sheer blouse. The thread work surrounding the lace and appliqués adds design interest and moves the eye along the skirt border (below).

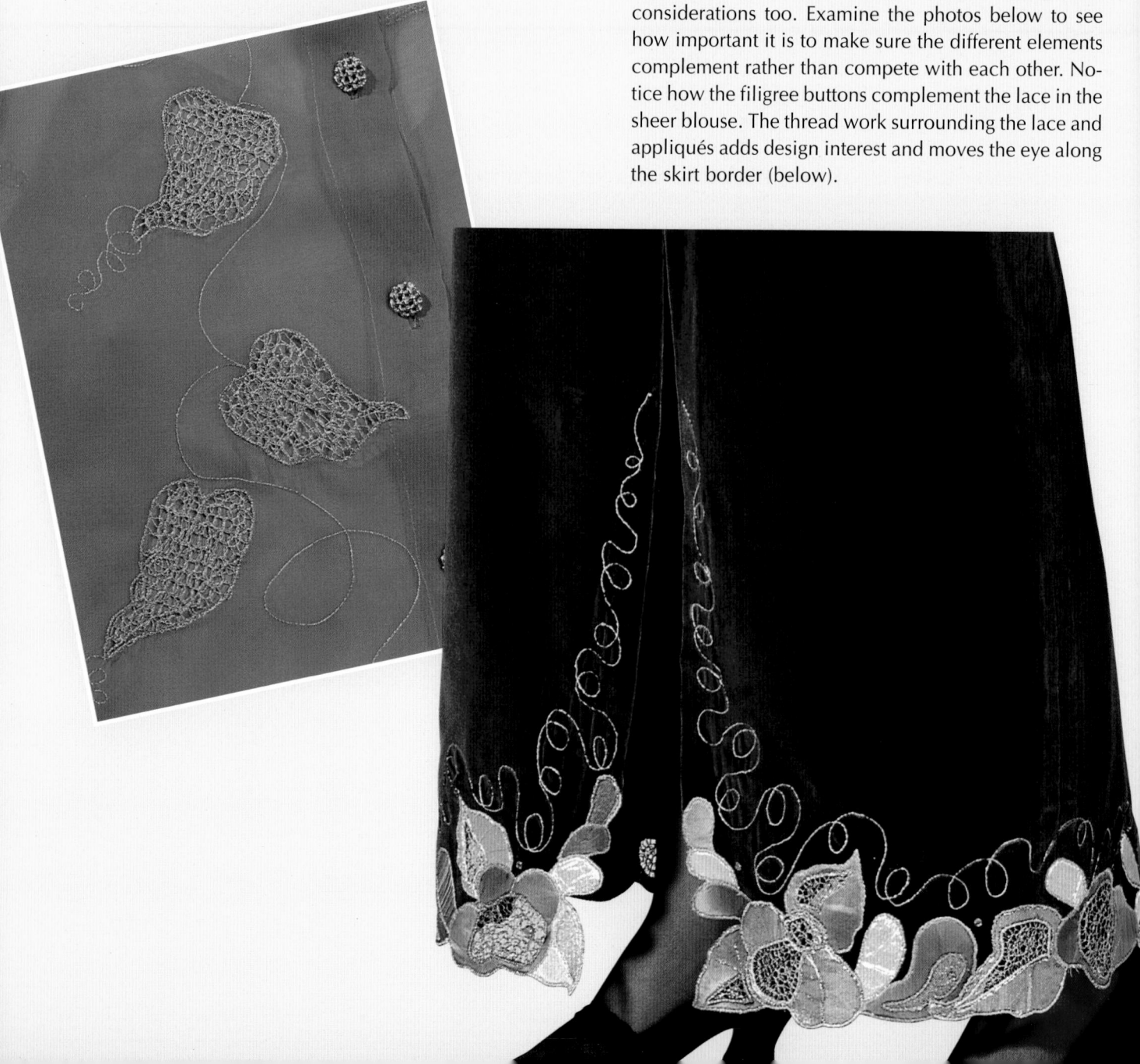

❧ For continuity, add interest to smaller areas. Sleeves, collars, and cuffs are perfect places for integrating design motifs used elsewhere in a garment.

❧ Use the element of surprise. In the detail of the tunic shown below, one might expect to find an actual bow at the neckline. Instead, I used a bow appliqué. The button in the center serves as a "knot" as well as a functional neckline closure.

❧ Consider connected pattern pieces as one area, not as separate pieces. When they are sewn together, your eye perceives the pieces as one unit. The design should flow over rather than end abruptly at seam lines.

❧ If you adapt and adjust your design while creating it, you may end up with extra appliqués. Don't discard them. Instead, use them on the lining (if the garment has one) to make the garment even more interesting.

Placing the Design

Symmetrical designs have the same arrangement on each side of a central point. In other words, if you draw an imaginary line down the center, each side mirrors the other one.

Asymmetrical designs have an uneven distribution of design motifs. Opposite sides of the garment are different. These designs are more difficult to plan but, because they are unpredictable, usually result in more eye appeal.

Symmetrical Design Placement

Asymmetrical Design Placement

There are two basic design processes. You can use a paper pattern to create your design, or you can skip this step and design directly on a partially constructed garment (some major seams already stitched and pressed). Designing first with paper allows you to make adjustments to the main pieces before cutting into the fabric. Also, appliqué designs containing many parts can be photo-

copied and moved around for placement, remaining intact on a sheet of paper. Designing on fabric (skipping the paper step) locks you into the pattern; changes may not be possible once the garment has been cut and sewn.

Designing on Paper

To begin, position the design motifs on a flat surface where you can see them, such as a design wall. You should have several copies of the final design in both right and left (mirror-image) versions so you can play with placement and various motif combinations. Make copies of the design on clear acetate, then reverse the acetate on the copier to get a mirror image.

Next, place the design motifs on the paper pattern, moving the motifs around to find interesting groupings. Play with different arrangements until you find one you like; then pin the motifs in place on the paper pattern.

Designing with Lines

If the process described above seems intimidating and you don't know where to start, try dividing the pattern pieces with lines into geometric spaces. Lines appeal to our sense of structure and create placement guides for the design motifs. Later, you can remove the lines or, if you like the structure they provide, integrate them into the final design.

1. Draw horizontal and vertical lines on the paper pattern pieces. They should intersect like a trellis. Pin the design motifs in place so they appear to climb the trellis.

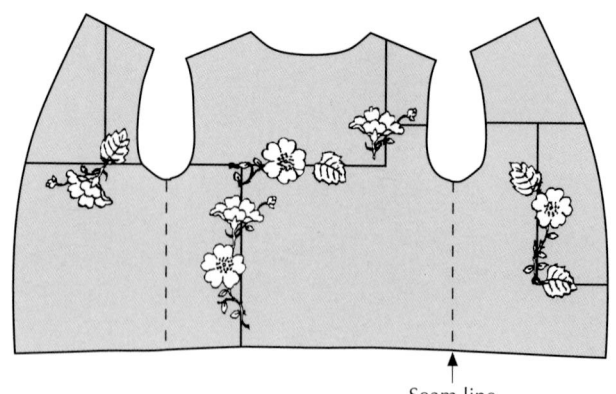

Seam line

You can also arrange design motifs by working from front to back and starting at the shoulder area, arranging a cluster of design motifs so they cascade down the garment.

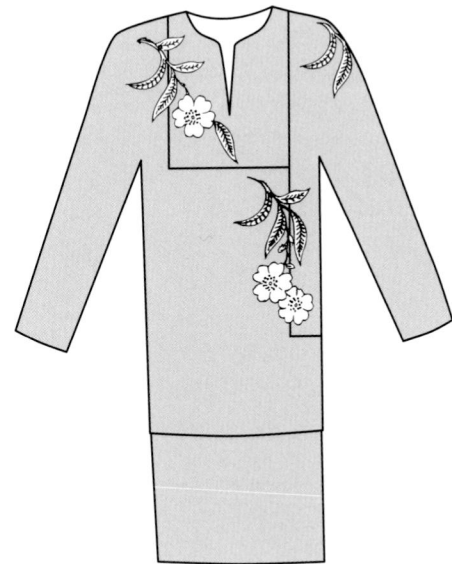

2. Continue the design motifs to the opposite front panel or on the back. This gives the piece movement and continuity. Allow the motifs to follow the lines of the garment so both work together. The rights and lefts of a design motif play an important role here. The shape of the pattern piece dictates whether a right- or left-oriented motif is more appropriate. If motifs have a natural curve, it is more pleasing to position them so they curve toward the garment center rather than away from it. This holds the viewer's eye within the garment rather than leading it away.

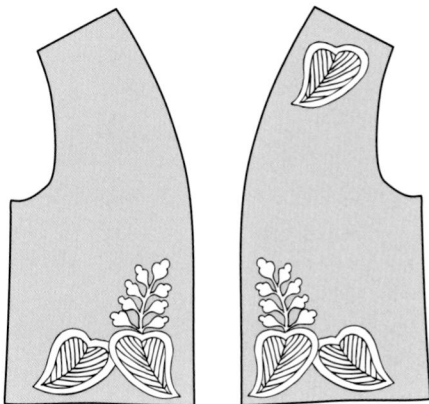

Eye-Pleasing Design Placement

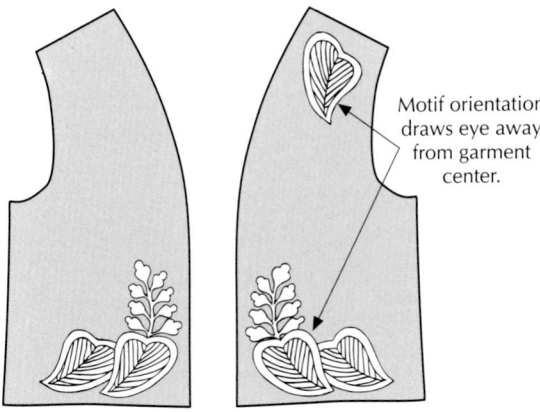

Motif orientation draws eye away from garment center.

Awkward Design Placement

3. Unpin the pattern pieces from the design wall and pin them together at the shoulder seams. Position the sleeves in their approximate location in the armhole areas as shown below. Arrange design motifs on the sleeves, embellishing one or both sleeves. If you embellish both sleeves, either create mirror images or vary the design on each sleeve.

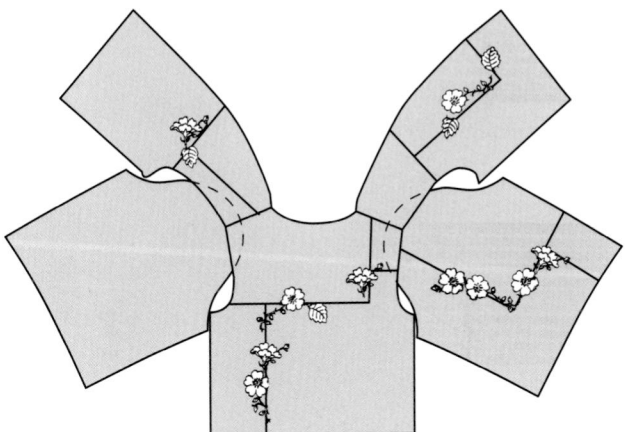

4. When you have achieved the desired effect, set the sleeves aside. With the shoulder seams still pinned, carefully try on the pattern and evaluate the design placement in relationship to your figure.
   - Is the overall placement appealing? Is it too cluttered or too sparse?
   - Are the motifs too close or too far apart?
   - Does the design flow without abrupt changes of direction that are distracting?
   - Are the shapes too large or too small?

   Play with design placement, size, and shape until you are satisfied.

5. Assemble the actual garment shell, sewing the side seams permanently. Don't sew the shoulder seams yet.

6. Transfer the design from paper to fabric. To do this, cut appliqué shapes from the desired fabrics and position them on the garment. Use the paper pattern as a placement guide.

Designing without a Pattern

When designing, it's OK to skip the paper pattern and go right to the fashion fabric, using fabric appliqués. You simply cut the main pattern pieces from the garment fabric and stitch the side seams, then pin the garment to the design wall and move the appliqué shapes around on the garment until you achieve the desired design.

ADDING PERMANENT FABRIC LINES

If you like the idea of using lines to define design areas (shown in the vest below), you can permanently apply lines, fusing narrow strips of fabric to the garment.

1. Apply paper-backed fusible web to the wrong side of a $1/4$-yard piece of appliqué fabric.

2. Rotary cut strips in the desired width from the fabric.

3. Remove the paper backing and position the strips on the garment as desired. Fuse in place before adding any other appliqués or design elements.

Note

Embellish the fabric strips with embroidery, using decorative machine stitches. Or, use a fabric marker to draw the strip widths on the appliqué fabric, and then embroider as desired (stitching through the backing paper). Rotary cut the strips from the fabric and fuse in place.

4. Finish the edges of the fabric strips with a decorative stitch.

5. Position the appliqués, then fuse and stitch them in place. (See "Positioning and Stabilizing the Appliqués" on page 36.)

Chapter 4

Machine Appliqué

Light in the Forest

Hand-painted silk charmeuse left over from a Fairfield Fashion Show garment found its way into this suit. The appliquéd flowers, inspired by some favorite tole-painting designs, cascade across the yoke and down the back of the smock-style silk noil jacket. A mixture of techniques—appliqué, needlelace, beading, bobbin work, and machine embroidery—combine to create a beautifully executed design.

*M*achine appliqué is the basis for most of the techniques in this book. It's used in conjunction with machine surface embellishment on both quilts and wearables.

There are several ways to machine stitch appliqués. The traditional method, using the satin stitch for a neat, strong finished edge, is probably the most familiar. It requires a traditional machine setup with a presser foot and with the feed dogs engaged.

An alternate method requires a free-motion setup. The resulting appliqués have a very soft edge because the machine stitching is less pronounced and definitive.

The stitches blend into the fabric, giving the illusion of being part of the appliqué itself.

The main purpose of the stitching is to hold the appliqué in place. The stitching is not a major design element in itself, but is there to support the focal point—usually another form of surface embellishment. Use the narrowest satin stitch possible to keep the stitching in the background, but use one wide enough to secure the appliqués.

Experiment with each method to see how each one handles on your particular fabric and design. There are differences; determine your own preferences.

MACHINE-APPLIQUÉ BASICS

- ❧ Use a machine-embroidery or appliqué needle, especially when using decorative threads.
- ❧ Apply liquid silicone to the spool to make the thread more manageable.
- ❧ Loosen the upper tension to prevent thread breakage.
- ❧ Stitch appliqués that lie underneath other appliqués first, regardless of which stitching method you use.
- ❧ Practice first with a sample appliqué. Try both stitching methods (satin stitch or free-motion straight stitching) to determine which is best for your needs.

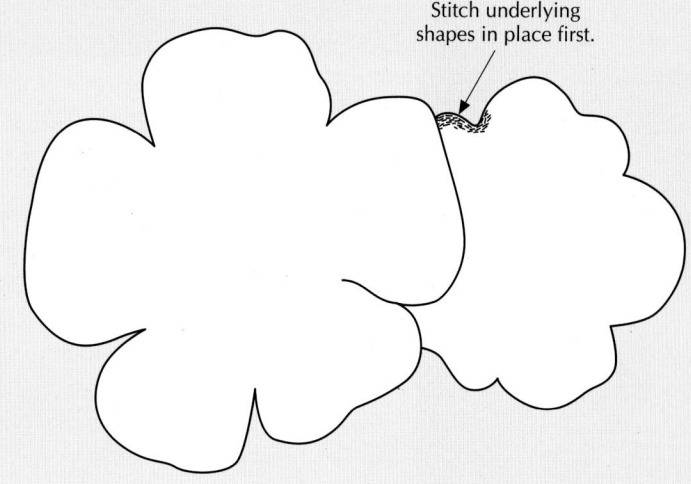

Stitch underlying shapes in place first.

Making Templates

You will need a clear plastic template for each shape in your appliqué design. Check at your fabric or quilt store for template material. My favorite is the clear vinyl report cover or vinyl envelope available at office-supply stores. This sturdy material is clear enough so you can see the appliqué fabric underneath, giving you the opportunity to control the color placement within each shape for the most effective and realistic results.

To make appliqué templates:

1. Using a fine-line, permanent black marker, trace each shape onto clear template material. Trace any detail lines that you will add with stitching later. If the motif is made up of many smaller pieces, such as a flower with lots of petals, trace each piece separately. Number each piece *and* the master paper pattern for easy reference.

2. Study the design and mark each template for color placement, using L for light, M for medium, and D for dark areas. For example, if a flower motif features a dark center, mark the shapes that make up the center with a D so you will know to place them in darker areas of the selected appliqué fabric. You can also mark more than one color area on a simple appliqué template to create color movement within the shape. Color movement in simple shapes makes for a more effective and realistic finished design.

3. Cut out each shape along the drawn line, leaving a bit of the black line behind here and there so you can more easily see the outer edge of the template when you place it on top of the fabric.

Cutting and Preparing the Appliqués

1. Following the manufacturer's directions, back each of the selected appliqué fabrics with a layer of paper-backed fusible web.
2. Place the appliqué template face up on the right side of the appliqué fabric and move it around as desired for dark, medium, and light color placement. Use a fabric marking pen to trace around each template. For a reverse image, which is common in asymmetrical designs, place the template face down on the right side of the fabric.
3. Cut out each appliqué shape and remove the backing paper.

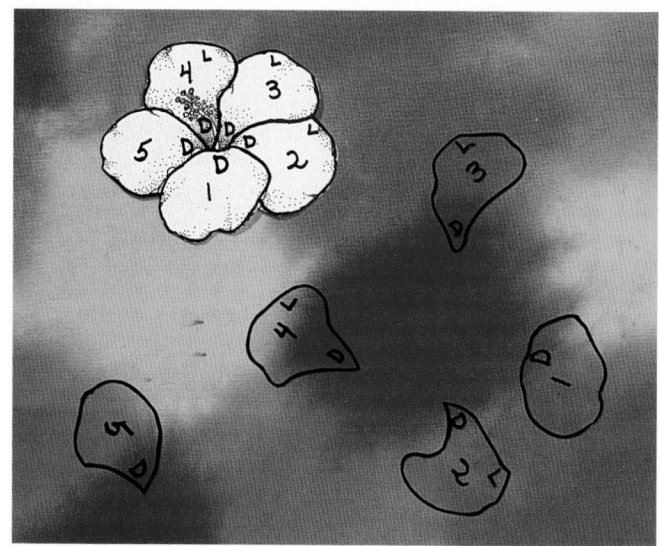

Positioning and Stabilizing the Appliqués

1. With the garment positioned on a large, flat surface, pin the prepared appliqué shapes in place. For exact positioning, place your prepared paper pattern on top of the garment and mark the placement. I usually eyeball this, unless the design elements must line up precisely across the garment, as in a mirror-image jacket or vest front. (See "Perfect Appliqué Placement" on page 37.)
2. With the appliqués pinned in place, pin the shoulder seams and try on the garment to evaluate the design before fusing. Make any necessary adjustments.
3. Following the manufacturer's directions and making sure the iron temperature is compatible with the appliqué and fashion fabric, fuse the appliqués in place. Use a pressing cloth if necessary.
4. Cut a piece of stabilizer slightly larger than the appliqué area. Iron or pin in place to the wrong side of the garment. Now you're ready to stitch the shapes, using your choice of two methods: traditional satin stitch (page 38) or free-motion straight stitching (page 40). But first, select thread for your work.

Choosing the Threads

Appliqué is beautifully enhanced with the decorative threads discussed in Chapter 2. Choose rayon or other decorative thread in a color to match the appliqué fabric and include a matching metallic or flat metallic thread as a highlight. If you have a multicolored appliqué fabric, use a decorative thread for each color. Or, determine the dominant color of the appliqué fabric and use that color only. To determine the dominant color, step back from the fabric and squint your eyes; the dominant color is sure to pop out at you.

A clear or smoke-colored transparent thread is acceptable for the bobbin, as is one of the special bobbin threads discussed on page 20. You can also work with regular sewing thread that matches the color of your decorative thread. Experiment to find the best one for your needs.

PERFECT APPLIQUÉ PLACEMENT

If your design is symmetrical, you might find it challenging to create precise mirror images. To achieve this, I have devised a simple trick. You'll need gluestick and double-stick cellophane tape.

1. Plan one side of the garment and fuse the appliqués in place. Place a small piece of double-stick cellophane tape on top of each fused piece.

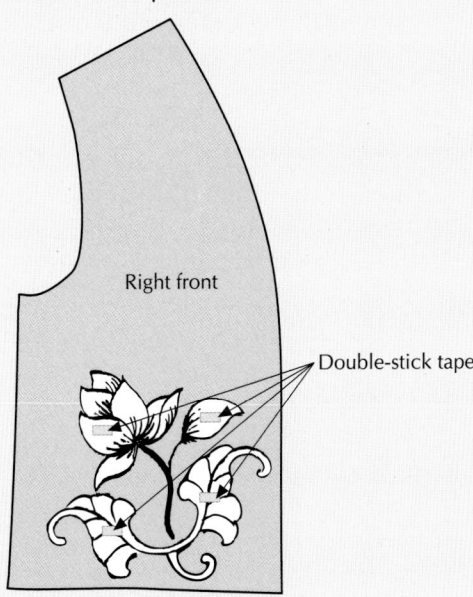

Right front

Double-stick tape

2. Apply paper-backed fusible web to the *wrong* side of each mirror-image appliqué. Remove the paper backing from each shape.
3. Position each shape face down on its matching fused shape; adjust so the edges are perfectly aligned. Apply pressure so the double-stick tape adheres to both shapes.
4. Using the gluestick, apply a bit of glue to the fusible web of each unfused shape.

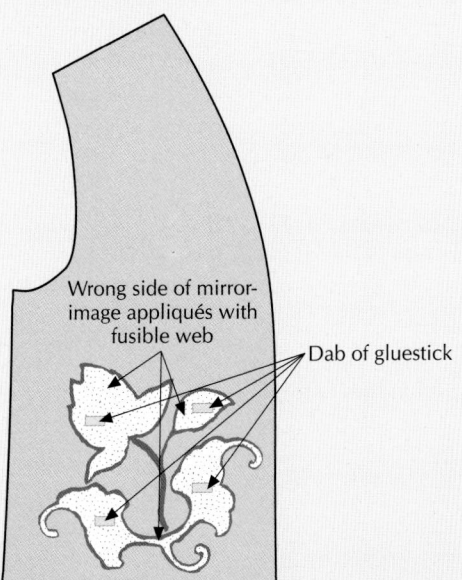

Wrong side of mirror-image appliqués with fusible web

Dab of gluestick

5. Place the remaining garment piece face down on top of the appliqué shapes. Align the cut edges of both garment pieces and firmly press the appliqués so the glue on each one adheres to the top garment piece.

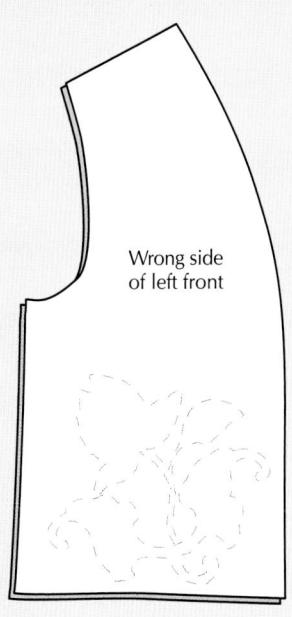

Wrong side of left front

6. Carefully peel back the top garment piece, making sure the appliqués remain in place while you remove the double-stick tape between the fused and unfused appliqués. You will have an exact mirror image. Before fusing the shapes in place permanently, adjust the appliqués as needed so those that will lie underneath others are correctly positioned.

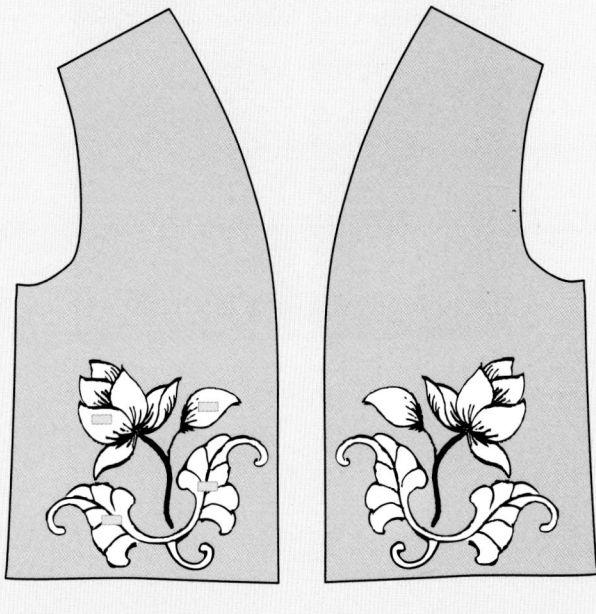

Satin Stitching

Set up your machine for traditional sewing, with the feed dogs up. Replace the all-purpose presser foot with the satin-stitch, appliqué, or open-toe embroidery foot. Adjust the stitch width to between 1mm and 2mm, and the stitch length to about 0.5mm. The stitch must be long enough for the fabric to feed through the machine without stitches piling up on each other. Before sewing the pieces in place, adjust the satin stitch as follows:

1. Thread your machine with the same type of threads you plan to use in your project. Use contrasting colors; do not use transparent thread.

2. Use a contrasting solid-color fabric with a stabilizer on the underside. I prefer iron-on, tear-away stabilizer for satin-stitch appliqué.

3. Stitch through the stabilized fabric for 2", then check the underside of the stitching. The top thread should show on the wrong side of the work. The ideal satin stitch has a slightly unbalanced tension with more pull coming from the bobbin. This eliminates the possibility of any bobbin thread showing on the right side. The wrong side should show a solid line of color from the bobbin with the top thread shadowing each side.

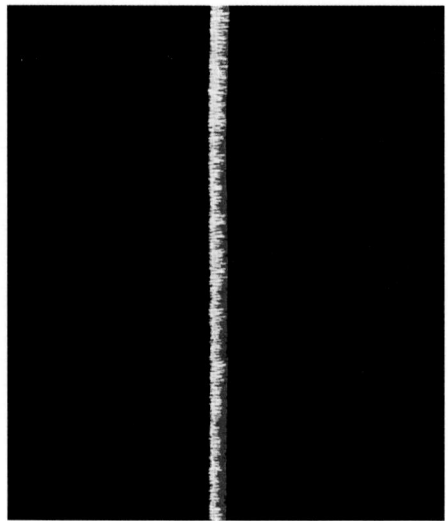

If your stitching does not look like this, try loosening the upper tension. Stitch again for 2" and recheck the stitch. Continue adjusting as needed. If necessary, tighten the bobbin tension to draw the top thread to the underside of your work. To do so, use a small screwdriver to turn the tension screw in the bobbin-case area. Check your owner's manual for more details.

Check the right side. The perfect satin stitch for appliqué is closely spaced so the fabric doesn't show through the stitches. It is also just long enough so there are no stitch-feeding and pileup problems. The goal is a smooth, nonlumpy outline on the right side.

4. When you are happy with the stitching, change threads and proceed with the satin stitching on your project. You may need to fine-tune the stitch a bit, depending on the threads you are using.

5. Sew the first appliqué piece—the bottommost piece in the layered design—in place. To begin stitching, hold the top thread in one hand and turn the handwheel toward you to bring the bobbin thread to the top. Position the needle so it will take the first stitch to the right of the appliqué edge, then swing over the edge and into the appliqué. Lower the presser foot and, holding the thread tails as you start, satin-stitch around the edge to secure the appliqué. (See "Satin Stitching Curves, Corners, and Points" on page 39.) Pull the threads to the underside and tie off securely. Clip thread tails to ½".

SATIN STITCHING CURVES, CORNERS, AND POINTS

The position of each satin stitch on the appliqué is important. You must constantly stop and turn or pivot the work as you go so each stitch is perpendicular to the appliqué edge. There are some special maneuvers you need to know to satin-stitch smoothly around curves, corners, and points.

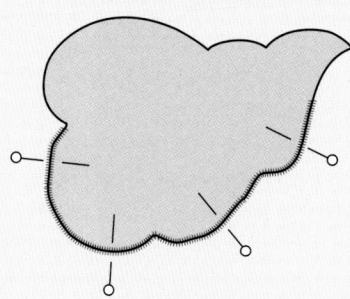

Curves

Satin stitching around curves requires frequent stops and starts.

To pivot on an outside curve:

1. Stitch until the stitching is no longer perpendicular to the appliqué edge. Stop with the needle in the garment fabric, outside the appliqué.
2. Raise the presser foot and pivot the fabric slightly so the stitching will be perpendicular to the appliqué edge. Lower the foot and continue in the same manner, stopping to adjust when the stitches are not perpendicular. This ensures a smooth line of satin stitching.

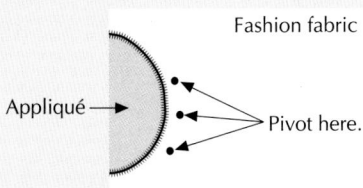

Fashion fabric

Appliqué →

Pivot here.

To pivot on an inside curve:

1. When the stitches are no longer perpendicular to the appliqué edge, stop stitching with the needle in the appliqué, one stitch width from the edge.
2. Raise the foot and pivot slightly so the stitching will be perpendicular to the appliqué edge. Lower the foot and continue stitching, stopping to adjust as necessary.

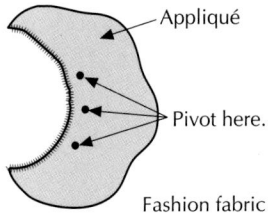

Appliqué

Pivot here.

Fashion fabric

Corners

1. Stitch to within ⅛" of the corner of the appliqué.
2. Swing the needle to the outside edge of the appliqué, making sure it is in the garment fabric.
3. Raise the presser foot and pivot the garment 90°.
4. Lower the foot and continue stitching along the next edge of the appliqué.

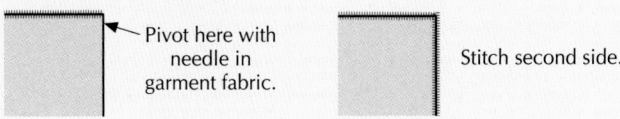

Pivot here with needle in garment fabric.

Stitch second side.

Points

To satin-stitch an inside point:

1. Stitch to the bottom of the V as deep as the width of the stitching. Stop with the needle in the appliqué, one stitch width from the edge.
2. Pivot and continue stitching along the next side.

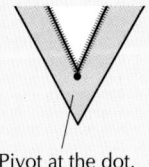

Pivot at the dot.

Satin stitching a sharp outside point requires a gradual change in the stitch width as you approach the point.

To satin-stitch a sharp outside point:

1. Make note of the zigzag width before you begin. Stitch along the first side, toward the point, until the stitch reaches across the appliqué, then gradually decrease the stitch width to almost 0. Stop with the needle down, to the right of the appliqué edge, and pivot.
2. Continue to stitch along the next side, gradually increasing the stitch width to the original setting.

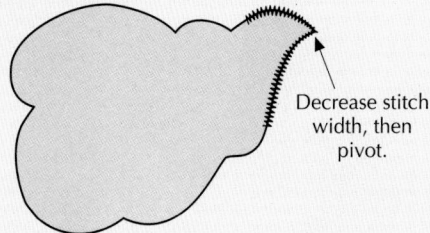

Decrease stitch width, then pivot.

Free-Motion Straight Stitching

I developed this form of machine appliqué many years ago when working on a quilt. I needed to machine stitch the appliqués because they had been fused, eliminating the possibility of hand stitching. I wanted a soft look at the edges to avoid drawing attention to the stitches. Much experimentation brought me to the following technique.

For this method, use a free-motion setup and a straight stitch. This method is more time-consuming because the straight stitch doesn't cover ground as quickly as satin stitching. However, it's easy and produces beautiful results. I enjoy this method because it creates an edge that blends with the appliqué. The stitching enhances without overpowering. It's also easy to use in conjunction with other techniques.

Setting Up the Machine

Unlike traditional sewing, free-motion stitching allows you to move the fabric in any direction under the presser foot. You control the direction in which the fabric moves rather than the feed dogs. You must lower or disengage the feed dogs and eliminate the pressure on the top of the fabric that is normally exerted by a traditional presser foot. If you cannot lower or disengage the feed dogs on your machine, use a feed-dog cover. If your machine requires a feed-dog cover, you may find it cumbersome. If that's the case, remove the cover and turn the stitch length to 0. Even though the feed dogs are exposed, they will not move.

You will need a darning foot. This special, spring-loaded foot is designed not to touch the throat plate when lowered into position. Some machines have a darning foot that does touch the throat plate. Adjust the pressure dial to the darning mode so the foot no longer touches the throat plate.

SEW SMART

The pressure dial is usually on the outside of the machine and controls the amount of pressure the presser foot exerts on the fabric. Do not confuse this dial with the tension dial, which controls tension on the upper thread. It's wise to check your manual to locate the pressure dial on your machine. Some machines do not have a pressure dial.

Many older machines don't come with a darning foot. For more play in the presser foot and optimum fabric maneuverability, use an appliqué foot and remove all pressure from the foot by turning the pressure dial to 0.

Some people enjoy doing free-motion sewing without any type of presser foot. This is an acceptable method, but you should be aware of some drawbacks. Having a foot on the machine gives you a point of reference. This makes it easy to see the needle position, reducing the possibility of catching your fingers in the needle. Using a foot is also an obvious reminder to lower the presser bar. If you don't lower the bar, your threads will tangle when you begin to stitch.

*To prepare the machine for free-motion
straight-stitch appliqué:*

1. Replace the all-purpose presser foot with the darning foot.
2. Lower or disengage the feed dogs.
3. Thread the machine with decorative thread on the top spool, and transparent thread or special bobbin thread in the bobbin.
4. Insert a fresh embroidery needle or a special metal needle if using metallic thread.
5. Decrease the upper tension by one number to create an uneven balance of tension in the top and bottom threads.

Stitching

Since this is probably a new method of sewing for you, be sure to practice first with scraps of your appliqué and garment fabric. It's not difficult, and a little practice is all it takes to develop your own technique.

1. Prepare the appliqués and garment as described for satin-stitched appliqués on page 36. When using this method, take care to fuse the appliqué edges completely to prevent them from popping up during stitching.
2. To begin stitching an appliqué in place, choose a point where another appliqué touches or overlaps it.
3. To take the first stitch, hold the top thread and turn the handwheel toward you, bringing the bobbin thread to the top. Hold both thread tails securely and begin sewing a series of very small, straight stitches. They resemble dots with a very illegible stitch length. In order to achieve this, it's necessary to run the machine quickly while moving the fabric slowly.
4. Work in small areas, no larger than ½" in size, and complete the stitching before moving to the next area. Do not stitch around and around the appliqué piece. This gives the appearance of rows or lines of stitching. Instead, you want to create the look of small dots of thread at the appliqué edge.

Allow some of the stitches to fall farther into the appliqué than others for a softer, freer look. The stitches appear to melt into the appliqué, and the edge is softer because of the lack of even stitching around it. Unlike traditional satin-stitch appliqué, this method does not require you to keep the stitches perpendicular to the appliqué edge. There is no real stitch direction because you are creating a series of little dots. (See the photo on page 42.)

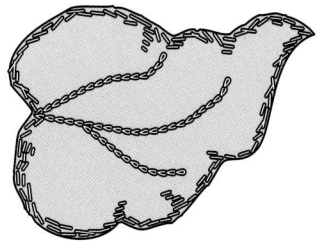

Free-motion straight stitching
results in a softer edge.
(Stitches are shown larger than normal.)

5. Continue stitching around the appliqué, ½" at a time. When finished, lock the stitches by taking a few stitches in place along the outer edge of the appliqué. Trim the thread close to the stitching.
6. If you find loose edges or threads along the completed appliqués—I call them "pokies"—trim them as close to the stitching as possible, using appliqué scissors.

Color Melting Your Threads

If you've chosen an appliqué fabric with lots of color movement, you might need to use more than one color of thread while stitching. In this case, stitch the areas requiring the first thread color in each appliqué. Rethread the machine with the next color and stitch the appropriate areas. Continue with additional thread colors as needed to complete the appliqué.

To avoid creating a sharp color line where two colors butt, I developed a technique I call color melting.

To color melt with thread:

1. Stitch with the first thread color in appropriate areas of the appliqué, and continue stitching into the next color area. Take a few stitches, even though it is not the thread color you intend to use there.
2. Change to the next thread color and start stitching in the color area you just completed, taking a few stitches there, and then continuing into the second area. Extend for a few stitches into the third area.

This subtle mixing of thread color at the beginning and end of each area prevents sharp color changes and is more pleasing to the eye.

PRACTICE MAKES PERFECT

If you have limited machine-appliqué experience, it's beneficial to try free-motion stitching on paper first. I call this paper doodling. Working through this exercise will help you get the feel for the technique before you sit down to sew. It reminds me of stitching exercises I did as a middle-school student in home economics class.

1. Draw any appliqué shape on a piece of paper.
2. Using a pencil, pretend you are appliquéing this shape. Simulate a free-motion machine stitch on the paper as described on page 41. Notice the stitch in relationship to the edge of the appliqué shape.
3. Draw the same shape on another sheet of paper and repeat the exercise, this time using your pencil to draw the traditional satin stitching. Notice that you must stop and turn the appliqué to keep the stitches perpendicular to the edge.
4. Using one of your still-good-but-not-new machine needles, try both stitching techniques on paper *without* thread.

Chapter 5
Needlelace Basics

Sunshine on My Shoulders

Sun-drenched primary and secondary colors shout "Don't miss me!" in this jacket and dress ensemble. Reminiscent of "South of the Border" color and design, each leaf and flower in the border features machine needlelace worked in rayon and metallic embroidery threads. Bobbin-work tendrils play a unifying role, connecting scattered leaves to the border treatment.

*M*achine needlelace adds interest and beauty to garments and quilts. You can use it in a number of exciting ways to enhance other embellishments. I love to make a bit of lace inside an appliqué shape for added texture and eye appeal. I also make needlelace directly on the garment without appliqués. Lace inside an appliqué adds more color; lace without appliqués is more subtle.

Before making needlelace, you will need to prepare the garment and appliqués and choose the appropriate threads. To help you learn how to make needlelace, I have provided a practice pattern. Use it to make appliqués that will have lace in the interior, or trace the shape directly onto fashion fabric and make lace without an

appliqué. It's a good idea to practice on scraps and make reference samples before embarking on your first project.

Needlelace-in-Appliqué

You will need the following materials to make a needlelace-in-appliqué sample. If you prefer to dig in and make needlelace for a project—a vest, blouse, or jacket, for example—you will need to adjust the fashion-fabric, appliqué-fabric and fusible-web yardage requirements. Consult the back of your pattern envelope.

Materials

Needlelace pattern on page 92.
½ yd. muslin (or solid-color fashion
fabric if making a garment)
Fabric scrap for appliqué
Scrap of paper-backed fusible web
Small piece of tear-away stabilizer
Water-soluble stabilizer
Rayon machine-embroidery thread
to match appliqué fabric
Metallic machine-embroidery thread to
blend with rayon thread
Transparent nylon or polyester thread
7"-diameter spring embroidery hoop
Scraps of fabric to back needlelace
Embroidery scissors
Fabric marker

Getting Ready

1. If you are making a sample, cut an 18" square of muslin. Apply lightweight interfacing to the wrong side of the muslin for added support. (For a garment, cut the pattern pieces from the fashion fabric and set aside. Refer to the box below to determine whether you need to interface your fabric.)
2. If you are working on a garment, sew the fronts to the back at the side seams and press open. Staystitch around the entire outer edge of each garment piece.
3. Make templates for each appliqué shape required. (See "Making Templates" on page 35.) Back the appliqué fabrics with fusible web and cut the required shapes. (See "Cutting and Preparing the Appliqués" on page 36.)
4. Fuse and then stitch the appliqués in place using either a satin stitch or free-motion straight stitching.
5. Set up the machine for free-motion stitching, with a darning foot in place and the feed dogs lowered. (See "Free-Motion Straight Stitching" on pages 40–41.) Be sure to decrease the upper tension by one number if using decorative thread. You will use both straight and zigzag stitching.

DO YOU NEED AN INTERFACING?

Decorative machine work often requires more support than fashion fabric can provide. In that case, you will need to interface the garment section before you make the needlelace. Consider the following points to determine whether or not your fabric requires an extra layer of support.
❧ Does the fabric have a lot of give, as in a knit fabric?
❧ Is the fabric loosely woven or very limp to the touch?
❧ Will there be an extensive amount of embellishment and machine work applied to the fabric surface?

If you answered yes to any of these questions, follow the steps below to add interfacing to the appropriate garment pieces.
1. Use the pattern pieces to cut the appropriate shapes from a lightweight woven or tricot-knit fusible interfacing. If you wish, trim the seam allowances from the interfacing to eliminate unnecessary bulk.
2. Following the manufacturer's directions, fuse the interfacing to the wrong side of the garment pieces. (See "Interfacing" on page 18.)

◄ Graduation Days

Created for my daughter's graduation, this peach linen suit is an excellent example of how effective a tone-on-tone scheme can be. Extensive cutwork on the sleeves and jacket was done with a mix of fabric—all in the same color and closely related values—to add subtle elegance to the peach linen. Scattered seed beads and pearls add the finishing touch.

6. To mark the lace areas in the appliqués, open the garment out flat. Use a fabric marker to lightly sketch the lace areas where you want them. Mark areas in some or every appliqué throughout the design, or mark the areas in every other appliqué. The choice is yours.

When planning the shape of the lace area, remember that it is easier on the viewer's eye if the lace shape roughly follows the outer contours of the appliqué. If your appliqué fabric has exciting color movement, find the least interesting area and mark that part for the lace. Examine the appliqués in the photo below to get an idea of how to mark lace areas inside appliqués. The design shapes included on pages 92–94 are also a good reference when planning lace placement and shape within an appliqué.

7. Choose a thread for the lace. It can match or contrast with the appliqué, depending on the look you want. This technique sparkles when worked with metallic threads; lamé threads, such as Sliver; and rayon and silk threads.

8. Thread the bobbin with transparent thread or a thread that matches the top spool. Both sides of the lace are visible, so thread compatibility is important.

Making the Needlelace

1. Test your stitching first, using the same threads and stabilizer you will be using for your project. Using a spring hoop, place the stabilizer on top of the outer plastic ring of the spring hoop, followed by the appliqué right side up. Insert the inner ring of the hoop.

2. Set the machine for a free-motion straight stitch. Turn the handwheel while holding the top thread and take a stitch manually to bring the bobbin thread to the top, on the right side of the appliqué. Hold both the top and bobbin threads securely and take a few stitches to begin. Trim the thread tails.

3. Free-motion straight stitch (approximately 10 stitches per inch) around the lace outline. Don't worry about how the stitching looks; it only attaches the appliqué to the stabilizer. You will cover this stitching in the final step.

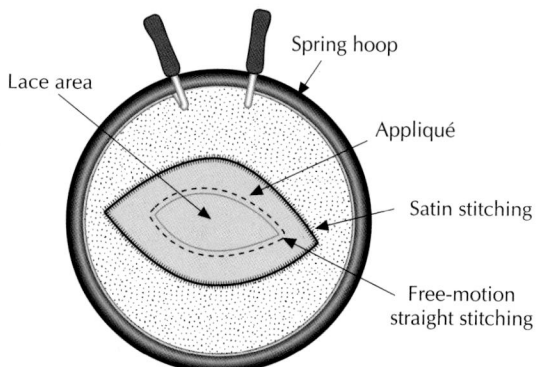

4. Remove the appliqué from the hoop and, using a pair of sharp embroidery scissors, cut away the appliqué fabric *inside* the stitching, leaving the stabilizer intact. Cut close to the stitched line—about ¹⁄₁₆"—taking care not to cut the stitching. Place the prepared appliqué back in the hoop with the appliqué face up as before.

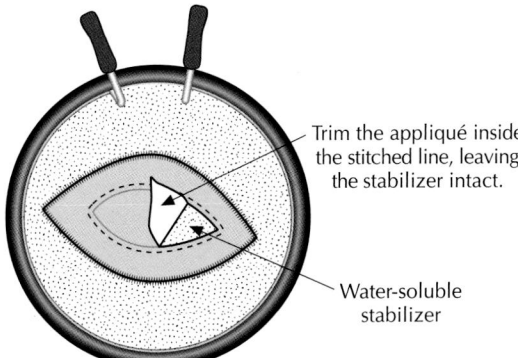

Trim the appliqué inside the stitched line, leaving the stabilizer intact.

Water-soluble stabilizer

5. Bring the bobbin thread to the right side, and with the machine set for a straight stitch, hold the thread tails while you take a few stitches near one edge of the fabric surrounding the stabilizer. Trim the tails close to the surface.

6. Start stitching in small circles the size of a pea, following the line of straight stitching. Overlap the circles as you go and make sure the needle catches the edge of the appliqué and fashion fabric. Continue to stitch in a series of overlapping circles. Remember, the circles must connect to other circles so, when the stabilizer is removed, the stitches form an interlocking web. Otherwise, you will have loose areas of lace.

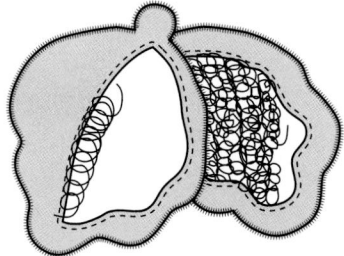

Beginning on one edge, fill in the stabilizer with circles of stitching.

7. Continue stitching interlocking circles until the open area is filled. Stitch back and forth, up and down, or in any direction as long as the circles interlock and those close to the edge catch the appliqué fabric.

If your circles look choppy, run the machine at high speed while slowly moving the hooped fabric.

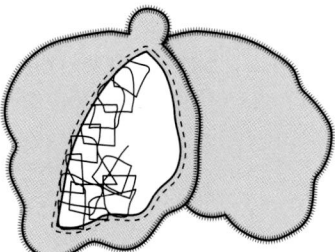

Correct choppy circles by running the machine quickly while moving the hooped fabric slowly.

8. Detail lines create interest as well as reinforce the lace. Stitch the detail lines along a line marked on the lace, or stitch them without any marking, relying on your eye to place and shape them. Refer to the appliqué pattern in either case. Use a fine-point, water-soluble marker to mark detail lines; fabric marking pencils are not fluid enough to mark on needlelace.

Free-form stitching the detail lines looks more natural. Close examination of leaf and flower veins reveals that lines are sporadic rather than perfectly placed. Relying on your eye for placement in the lace, rather than precisely measuring and marking the lines, results in a softer, more natural look.

9. Adjust the machine for a narrow zigzag stitch (1.5mm to 2mm). A narrow stitch enhances the needlelace; a wider stitch detracts from its delicacy. Bring the bobbin thread to the top and take a few stitches where the lace connects to the fabric.

10. Stitch along the detail line into the lace, connecting to the fabric edge at the opposite edge for added strength. Stitch additional lines, connecting them from fabric edge to fabric edge or from the central line to the fabric edge. If your free-motion stitching is not perfect, you can always go back over the line a second time to fill it in or neaten it. Add detail lines to the appliqué in the same manner. Refer to the illustration at the top of page 48.

11. Without changing the machine setting, bring the bobbin thread to the top and secure as before. Hold both thread tails and free-motion satin-stitch over the fabric edges to cover the first line of straight stitching.

Begin at any point on the edge and continue around until it is totally enclosed with stitches. As with regular satin stitching, *you must constantly move the piece to keep the stitches perpendicular to the fabric edge*. This is actually easier in free-motion work because *you* have control of the movement, not the feed dogs.

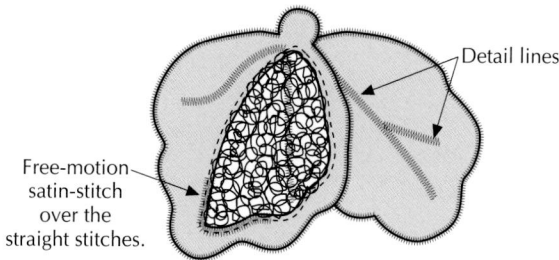

Free-motion satin-stitch over the straight stitches.

Detail lines

12. Remove the fabric from the hoop and trim any excess stabilizer beyond the stitched area on the underside of the work. For water-soluble stabilizer, hold the fabric in a V shape *with the stabilizer on the bottom to prevent the dissolving stabilizer from running back into the fabric*. Position the appliqué opening under slowly running tap water; avoid wetting the rest of the fabric if possible. Stabilizer left in, although not harmful or permanent, will stiffen the fabric.

When removing water-soluble stabilizer from nonwashable fabric, the process is less aggressive. Carefully pour a small amount of water from a spouted cup into the center of the lace and allow the water to trickle through. Be careful not to wet the fabric. You can also try ironing the lace between two moistened pressing cloths or paper towels. The moisture will remove the stabilizer. A wet sponge dabbed on the lace works too. Both of these processes must be repeated several times to ensure complete removal.

For a heat-disintegrating stabilizer, follow the manufacturer's instructions, observing caution with heat-sensitive threads and fabrics. Using a very thin pressing cloth is helpful for this type of removal.

A STITCH IN TIME SAVES LACE

After removing the stabilizer, any unconnected circles of stitching are easy to mend. Simply slip a small piece of stabilizer under the problem area and take a few circular stitches to connect the loose circles. Remove the stabilizer.

Backing the Needlelace

Needlelace is beautiful by itself when used as an edge finish or a border on sleeves, vests, and jackets. Needlelace used in other areas, such as bodices and jackets, often requires a backing fabric. The delicate lace shouldn't compete with the clothing worn underneath it. If lining a garment treated with lace, you'll need to back the lace before adding the lining.

1. Decide on a backing fabric. You can use the appliqué fabric, the fashion fabric, or an entirely different fabric. Needlelace has a subtle appearance when you back it with fabric in the same color as the appliqué and lace, and it becomes more prominent when you use a contrasting fabric. For a glitzy touch, try a shiny fabric, such as satin, tricot lamé, or tissue lamé.

2. Turn the garment to the wrong side and cut a piece of backing fabric 1" larger all around than the lace opening. Use pins to secure the backing behind the lace. Put the piece into the hoop with the appliqué on top and the backing fabric on the bottom.

3. Free-motion straight stitch around the opening edge, following the last line of stitching and using matching thread. This step is comparable to stitching in-the-ditch.

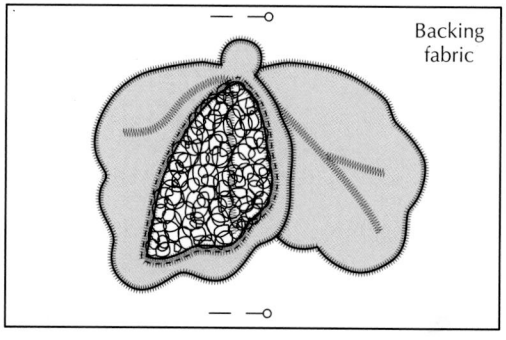

Backing fabric

Stitch in-the-ditch along the inner edge of the satin stitching.

4. Remove the fabric from the hoop and turn it to the wrong side. Trim the backing fabric to within ½" of the stitched line. If the backing fabric is prone to

fraying, treat it with a liquid seam sealant, such as FrayCheck.

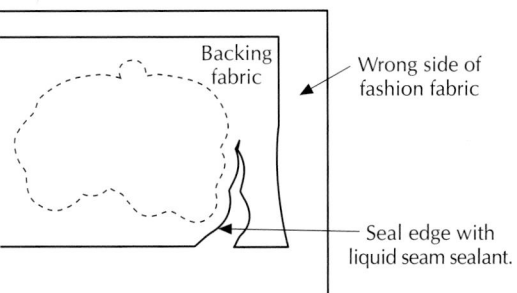

Backing fabric

Wrong side of fashion fabric

Seal edge with liquid seam sealant.

5. Complete all the appliqués and finish the needlelace inside those appliqués where you want it. Follow the pattern directions to complete the garment.

Backing the needlelace with the same fabric as the garment creates an effect I call shadowing. The lace is worked without an appliqué, eliminating added color. The photo at right shows a lacy fern made this way. The fern was created by tracing the appliqué shape onto the fashion fabric, making the needlelace inside the shape, and then backing it with a scrap of the same linen used for the jacket.

Needlelace without Appliqué

This variation of needlelace is more refined because of the absence of the appliqué piece. For this variation, make a sample or choose a simple pattern and try your hand on an actual garment. Use the pattern on page 92 for "Needlelace-in-Appliqué," or design one of your own. When referring to the instructions for "Needlelace-in-Appliqué," substitute "fashion fabric" for "appliqué."

Materials

Simple blouse pattern and solid-color fashion fabric in the yardage needed (or a small fabric square if you are only making a sample)
Water-soluble stabilizer
Cotton embroidery thread to match fashion or sample fabric
7"-diameter spring embroidery hoop
Embroidery scissors
Fabric marker

Making the Needlelace

1. Following the pattern instructions, cut the garment pieces from the fashion fabric. Staystitch around the raw edges. Stitch either the shoulder or side seams. (If you choose to put lace around a neckline, sewing the shoulder seams makes it easier. If you choose to use lace throughout the bodice, fronts, and backs, sewing the side seams is the best setup.)

2. Make templates for the design motifs as directed on page 35 for making appliqué templates. Place the templates right side up on the right side of the appropriate garment piece. Using a fabric marker, trace around the templates. Include detail lines.

3. Use cotton embroidery thread for the top spool and bobbin.

4. Set the machine for a free-motion straight stitch.

5. Cut a piece of stabilizer a little larger than the spring hoop and place it on top of the plastic outer ring. Layer the garment fabric on top, right side up, then insert the inner metal ring of the hoop.

6. Using a fabric marker, mark the areas for the lace.

7. Position the hoop under the needle and darning foot. Turn the handwheel while holding the top thread to bring the bobbin thread to the top. Hold both threads in one hand and take a few stitches. Trim the thread tails and continue to sew on the marked design line to attach the fabric to the stabilizer. This stitching doesn't have to be perfect; you will cover it later. If the shape is within another shape, stitch on the drawn lines to attach the fabric to the stabilizer underneath.

You can mark a portion of the design for lace (A) or do the whole design (B).

8. Remove the work from the hoop and use a pair of sharp embroidery scissors to trim fabric from inside the lace area. Cut close to the stitched line—about $\frac{1}{16}$" away—taking care not to cut the stitching. Leave the stabilizer intact.

9. Stitch the lace as directed for "Needlelace-in-Appliqué" on page 45. Add detail lines to the lace and/or in the garment within the stitched outline of the design.

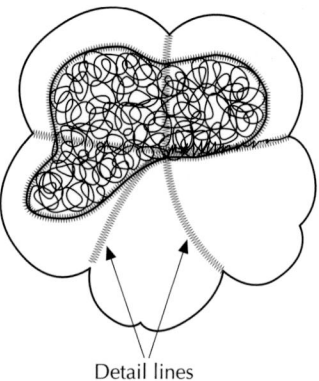

Detail lines

10. Satin-stitch over the outline stitching of each design shape.

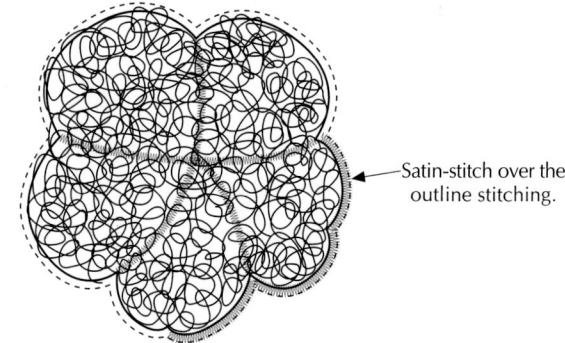

Satin-stitch over the outline stitching.

11. Referring to step 12 on page 48, remove the stabilizer.

12. Back the lace with another fabric as described on pages 48–49, or leave it open for a peek-a-boo look.

Chapter 6

Specialty Fabrics

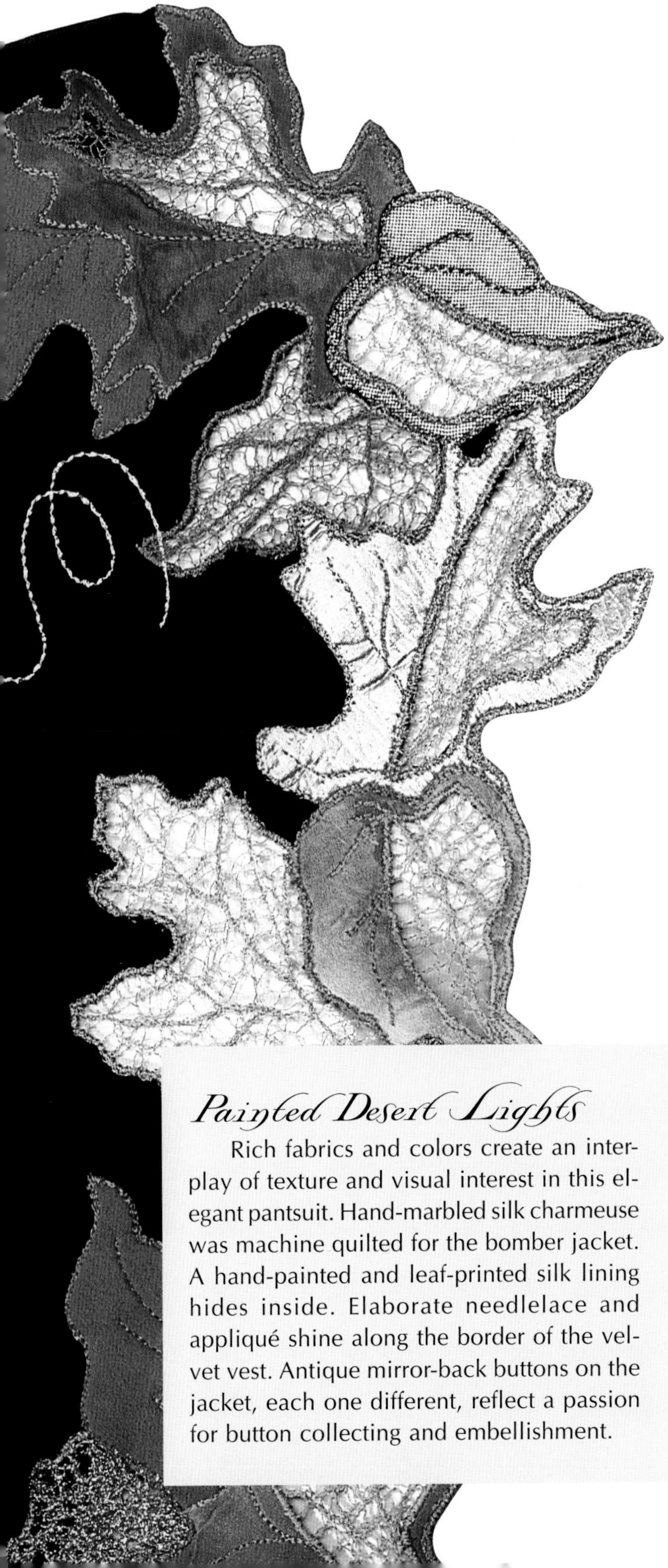

Painted Desert Lights

Rich fabrics and colors create an interplay of texture and visual interest in this elegant pantsuit. Hand-marbled silk charmeuse was machine quilted for the bomber jacket. A hand-painted and leaf-printed silk lining hides inside. Elaborate needlelace and appliqué shine along the border of the velvet vest. Antique mirror-back buttons on the jacket, each one different, reflect a passion for button collecting and embellishment.

*T*here are many beautiful fabrics suitable for appliqué and needlelace techniques. Some, however, require additional measures to make them workable.

Knits

Because knit fabrics stretch, they are not always considered ideal for certain forms of machine work. If you add lightweight fusible tricot-knit or woven interfacing to stabilize the stretch, you will be able to embellish these fabrics too. (See "Interfacing" on page 18.)

Pile Fabrics

Some of the heavier, luxurious fabrics are perfect for evening wear. These garments are ideal candidates for lace embellishment. For example, the richness of velveteen is complemented by delicate lace; worked in metallic thread, it's even more exciting.

Corduroy is wonderful when coupled with lace and other machine techniques. This fabric is usually reserved for more casual styles, so plan the design accordingly.

Pile fabrics, such as velveteen and corduroy, fray extensively, and the fraying threads can get caught in the stitching, creating havoc with the lace. Appliqué pieces used with the lacework help to stabilize the raw edges, but noticeable fraying still occurs. Besides, appliqué is not always appropriate in the design. As an alternative, treat raw edges with a liquid seam sealant, such as FrayCheck, before stitching the lace. Allow the sealant to dry at least 15 to 20 minutes after application so there is no chance of it dissolving your water-soluble stabilizer.

Sheers

Needlelace is beautiful in sheer fabrics, such as organza, silk, synthetic chiffon, and lightweight silk, but sometimes the fabric is not strong enough to support the threadwork. The thin, delicate fibers can pull away from an embellished edge, creating a hole as shown in the photo at right. An application of seam sealant along the cut edges of these fabrics adds strength and keeps the lace and fabric from separating. (For how-tos, see the practice project on page 53.)

Tapestry

Tapestry is fascinating fabric and a personal favorite of mine. Its designs are rich in texture and color. I scour the interior-design section of fabric stores for tapestry destined for walls and furniture, and then make it into clothing instead.

This expensive fabric is usually heavier and stiffer than most garment fabrics. Even with these drawbacks, I have great success using it for simple, straight-line garments—jackets and vests in particular. It's fun to try needlelace and other machine techniques in tapestry, because the results are elegant and unique. Just remember not to overdo the embellishment; you don't want it to overshadow the beauty of the tapestry.

As a rule, tapestry is tightly woven, so you can usually eliminate precautions taken with other heavier fabrics that do fray. Be guided by the behavior of your individual piece of fabric.

Synthetic Suede

I love to use a little synthetic suede in my work. It is available in two weights; the heavier one has less drape. Both weights are appropriate for garments, and needlelace is a wonderful complement. Synthetic suede does not fray, a real plus when it comes to appliqué work. Straight stitching is all it takes to hold suede shapes in place, but you can play with decorative stitches too.

Synthetic suede is expensive, so if you are a bit cautious about using it, try it first in small areas. For example, it makes a great accent fabric for collars and cuffs. Of course, it doesn't take much suede to make an appliqué or two like those in Mushroom Medley, shown at right. Some fabric and crafts stores sell it in small squares for this purpose.

Practice Project: Sheer Lace Butterfly Scarf

You will need to make some adjustments to the needlelace procedure when working with sheer fabrics. For this project, use a metallic thread on top and in the bobbin. When the lace is obvious on both sides, it's important to use the same thread in both places, or use two compatible decorative threads. A size 11/80 machine-embroidery needle handles the metallic thread and is gentle on the delicate fabrics.

Materials

Butterfly pattern on page 91.
⅜ yd. sheer, very drapable fabric, such as silk or synthetic chiffon for scarf*
Thread to match scarf fabric
1 spool metallic thread for butterfly
1 package water-soluble stabilizer
7"-diameter spring embroidery hoop
Size 11/80 machine-embroidery needle
FrayCheck and small paintbrush
Fabric marking pen
Use a purchased scarf if desired.

Directions

1. Cut a 10" x 45" strip of scarf fabric on the crosswise grain. (Tear it across the fabric width if it will not damage the fabric.)
2. Finish all raw edges with a narrow rolled edge on the serger or with a narrow rolled hem on the machine.

3. Adjust the machine for free-motion straight stitching as directed on pages 40–41. Use metallic thread for the top spool and bobbin.

4. Place one end of the scarf over the butterfly pattern and, using a fabric marking pen, lightly trace the design onto the fabric. Trace only the outline; do not trace detail lines.

5. Place the scarf in the spring hoop with the design centered. Place under the presser foot.

6. Holding the top thread, rotate the handwheel to bring the bobbin thread to the top. Hold both threads and take a few stitches. Trim the thread tails and continue to stitch on the marked line, using a free-motion straight stitch. Stitch the outer lines and body. Do not stitch the antennae.

7. Following the manufacturer's instructions, remove the fabric-marker markings. Paint a fine line of seam sealant inside the stitched line and a little beyond. Allow to dry thoroughly (usually 5 to 10 minutes), then remove the fabric from the hoop.

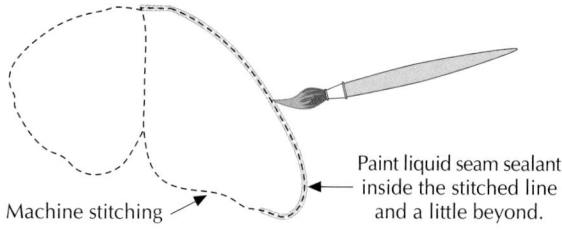

Machine stitching

Paint liquid seam sealant inside the stitched line and a little beyond.

PAINT THE EDGES

If you try to squeeze liquid sealant directly onto the fabric, you often end up with too much sealant, leaving unwanted marks on the fabric. To avoid this, squeeze some sealant into its cap and, using a tiny paintbrush the size of an eyeliner brush, paint the sealant onto the fabric.

8. Cut a piece of water-soluble stabilizer 1" larger all around than the hoop. Place the stabilizer in the hoop, then layer the fabric on top. Stitch around the design, following the previous stitched line.

9. Remove the work from the hoop and, using a pair of sharp embroidery scissors, trim the sheer fabric (not the stabilizer) ⅛" inside the stitched wing lines. Do

not trim the fabric inside the body section. Return the scarf to the hoop, keeping the design centered and taking care to prevent distortion.

10. Referring to "Needlelace-in-Appliqué" on pages 45–49, fill the wings with needlelace. Substitute "sheer fabric" for "appliqué" in the directions.

11. Fill the butterfly body with free-motion straight or zigzag stitching. Leaving the fabric intact adds extra body here.

12. Stitch the antennae with free-motion zigzag stitching. Turn the fabric so the stitch moves parallel to the marked lines.

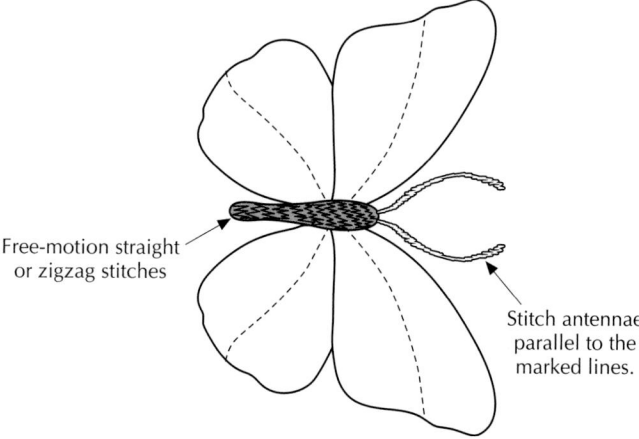

Free-motion straight or zigzag stitches

Stitch antennae parallel to the marked lines.

13. Carefully trim away the excess stabilizer and place the butterfly under gently running tap water to remove the remaining stabilizer.

14. For a more delicate look, add tiny seed beads to the needlelace. To do this, thread a beading needle or a size 12 Between needle with a piece of metallic thread. Hand sew the beads in place, taking a few stitches through the bead(s) and into the lace. Finish with a few stitches in place to secure the thread.

SEW SMART

As you learn about new techniques and/or threads, make small samples, noting tips, threads used, and the machine setup for each one. Store each sample in a separate plastic page protector and keep in a loose-leaf notebook. Use subject dividers to separate different categories, such as threads, fabrics, and water-soluble stabilizer techniques.

Chapter 7

Needlelace Borders

Poppies and Lace

Brightly colored poppies done in needlelace and as appliqués with needlelace accents pop boldly from the surface of this black silk noil garment. The collar, made completely of needlelace and appliqué, is the crowning jewel. Needlelace collar flounces, featuring rayon and metallic threads and couching yarns, were stitched on a heat-disintegrating stabilizer and the edges were trimmed with couched yarns.

*E*mbellishing borders with needlelace and appliqué is my favorite technique. Consider any garment edge a candidate for a needlelace border—the hem of a jacket and its sleeves, the hem of a skirt or dress, the outer edge of a collar, the top edge of a pocket, the overlapping edge of a wrap skirt, or the front edge of a blouse, jacket, or vest. Needlelace borders are also the perfect embellishment for small wall hangings.

The procedure for appliqué and needlelace borders is much the same as that described in "Needlelace Basics" on pages 43–50, but there are some differences. I have used a sleeve pattern to illustrate these changes. An appliqué pattern is provided on page 94, or use one of your own designs.

Autumn Splendor
Shaded appliqué and cutwork were used extensively on the jacket of this wool crepe outfit. Fall leaves were cut from hand-painted silk noil, then fused and appliquéd with rayon embroidery thread. Metallic thread adds another visual dimension to the needlelace accents and bobbin-work tendrils.

Designing a Border

When designing appliqués for a border, remember that you need to create a soft rather than a spiky or jarring edge. Use appliqué shapes with rounded edges as opposed to shapes with sharp or deeply curved edges. You also want to make sure the appliqués connect or overlap, so don't leave large negative spaces between shapes. All of these factors make for easier sewing and a more pleasing flow of design elements. Examine the two sleeves in the photo at right to better understand these principles.

Poor design with abrupt edges

Good design with pleasing flow

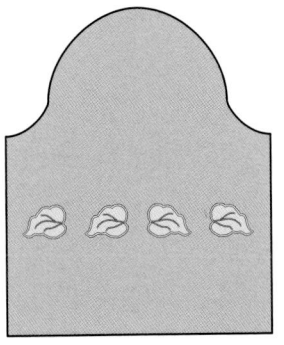

An appliqué design with negative or open space between shapes is not appropriate for borders.

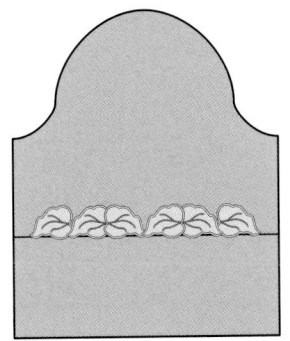

Connected and overlapped appliqués are easier to sew.

Stitching the Border

For best results, choose a jacket, blouse, or dress with a short, straight, set-in sleeve. Any sleeve will work, but a set-in sleeve hangs well and is ideal for supporting a lace border. A sleeve is used as an example, but you can make needlelace borders on other garment areas as well.

1. Following the pattern directions, cut out all the garment pieces except the sleeves.
2. Place the sleeve pattern on the fabric and add 4" to 5" of extra fabric beyond the finished hemline. (It's difficult to enclose appliqués in a hoop without this extra fabric, and since border treatments are obvious from both sides, it's important to use a hoop instead of tear-away stabilizer, which is difficult to remove completely.)
3. Lightly chalk-mark the hemline on the right side of the sleeve fabric. Turn up the fabric along the line and press lightly. Pin the underarm seam and try on the sleeve to make sure you are happy with the length. Adjust, if necessary, before making the needlelace border.

4. Referring to "Machine Appliqué" on pages 33–42, prepare the appliqués and place them so the bottom edge of each appliqué touches the marked hemline.
5. Fuse the appliqués in place, then satin-stitch the upper edge of each shape. Do not stitch along the lower edges.
6. Adjust the machine for a traditional or free-motion long zigzag stitch. Zigzag the lower edges of the appliqués to hold them in place for finishing.

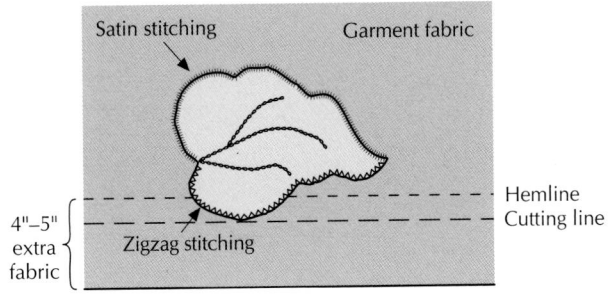

Satin stitching

Garment fabric

Hemline
Cutting line

4"–5" extra fabric

Zigzag stitching

7. Referring to "Needlelace-in-Appliqué" on pages 45–49, make needlelace as desired.

8. To finish the lower edge using a water-soluble stabilizer, trim excess fabric beyond the appliqués. Trim as close as you can without cutting the zigzag stitches. Secure a piece of stabilizer in a spring hoop. Place the appliquéd edge, right side up, over the stabilizer and pin in place. Satin-stitch the lower edge of the border. If there are several colors in the appliqué design, change threads as needed. When you come to the edge of the hoop, secure more stabilizer in the hoop and pin another section of the border in place for stitching. When the lower edge is complete, remove the stabilizer as described in step 12 on page 48.

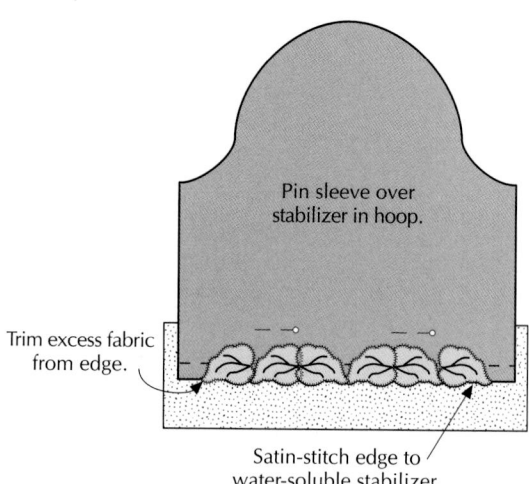

Pin sleeve over stabilizer in hoop.

Trim excess fabric from edge.

Satin-stitch edge to water-soluble stabilizer.

If you wish to add borders without appliqués, use a fabric marker and trace the design directly onto the fabric. Following the directions for "Needlelace without Appliqué" on pages 49–50 and using a traditional satin stitch, stitch the design lines and inside detail lines. Finish the edge as described above.

If you want to use motifs from printed fabrics to replace appliqué shapes in a border, choose a fabric with distinct design motifs, such as leaves. Back the fabric with fusible web, cut out the desired shapes, and apply them as you would appliqués. Secure the inner edges, add needlelace as desired, and finish the lower edges as described in step 8 on page 58.

Tone-on-tone fabric appliqués create an elegant border. To do this, you need a selection of fabrics in the same color and close value but with different surface textures. Choose fabrics that are close to the value and color of the fashion fabric.

Adding Borders to Curved Edges

Curved edges are also suitable for appliqué border treatments. The following directions are illustrated with a curved collar, but will work for any curved edge.

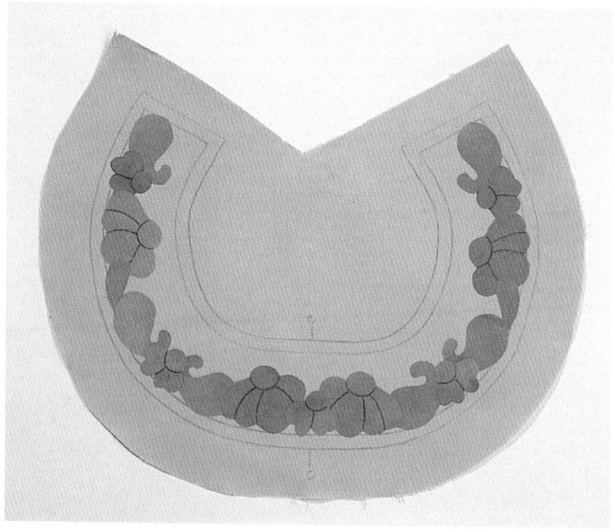

1. Cut a piece of fashion fabric several inches larger than the pattern piece all around so you can easily mount it in a hoop. Use a fabric marker to trace the pattern onto the fashion fabric. Mark the seam lines and cutting lines. Do not cut the collar from the fabric yet.

2. Prepare the appliqué shapes as described on page 36. As you position the shapes, remember that the entire collar edge does not need appliqués, but the ones you do use must connect to each other. If possible, place appliqués so they touch the seam line without extending beyond it. Fuse the pieces in place.

3. Cut a matching piece of fabric for the undercollar and a matching piece of paper-backed fusible web. Apply the fusible web to the wrong side of the prepared upper collar. Remove the paper backing and fuse to the *wrong* side of the undercollar. (The border is worked through both layers of the collar.)

4. Stitch the appliqués and add needlelace as directed for "Needlelace-in-Appliqué" on pages 45–48. Treat the bottom edge as discussed in step 8 on page 58. If areas of the collar have no appliqués, treat them as if they are the bottom edge of the appliqué, and satin-stitch. Don't forget to change thread colors as necessary.

Note

Handle faced edges, such as the front edge of a blouse, in the manner described for this collar, cutting two oversized fabric layers to fuse together. The fusible web and the weight of the appliqués add sufficient body, but you may want to use a lightweight fusible interfacing between the layers for additional support.

Using Borders in Lined Garments

4. Darken the *uppermost ridge line* on the rubbing. If the line needs to be softened into smoother curves, do so as you mark it. Sharp points and deep curves are difficult to finish.

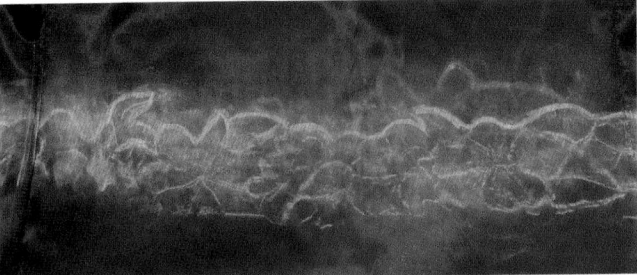

5. Remove the lining from the garment. Finish the hem with a balanced three-thread overlock stitch, serging on the marked line. If you don't have a serger, trim the lining ¾" below the marked line. Turn under and press a ⅜"-wide hem. Turn again and edgestitch.
6. Attach the lining and complete the garment, allowing the bottom edge of the lining to hang free.

Many garments require a lining to help them hang better, cover inner construction, or make them easier to slip on. Since you don't want a lining showing behind the lacework and since the placement of the lace areas varies, you can't simply cut a shorter lining.

1. Cut the lining according to the pattern instructions and assemble as directed.
2. *With wrong sides together*, pin the lining to the garment at the seam lines and around the armhole and neckline edges. Lay the garment as flat as possible, lining side up.
3. Using a piece of chalk in a contrasting color, rub the side of the chalk on the lining over the appliqué/lace area, much like you may have done a crayon and leaf rubbing when you were a child. The needlelace and appliqué stitch create a strong ridge—like the veins of a leaf—and rubbing with chalk will imprint them on the lining so you can see where the lace lies.

In a garment with a lined sleeve, hem the bottom edge of the lining in a straight line all around, making it just short enough to clear the lace. Allow the lining to hang free as shown in the inside view of the sleeve below.

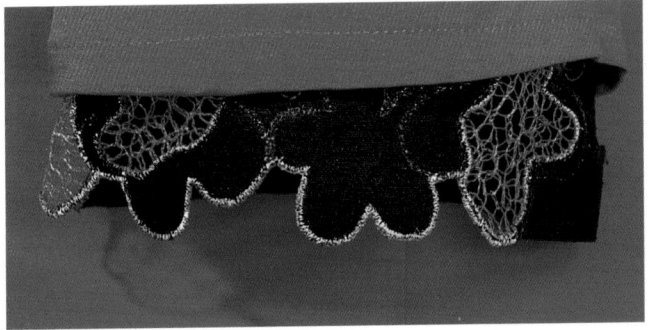

Adding Needlelace Borders to Quilts

Needlelace borders on quilted wall hangings are a beautiful alternative to traditional border treatments. The technique is similar to that used for clothing.

1. Mark the appliqué placement along the quilt edge as described for a garment on page 57.

2. Complete steps 4–6 as described for garment borders on page 57.

3. Mark the appliqué areas to be trimmed away for the lace. Choose areas in the appliqué fabrics with the least interesting color movement.

4. Cut the backing and batting pieces 3" to 4" larger than the bordered quilt top all around. Layer the quilt top with batting and backing; baste. Quilt by hand or machine out to *but not in* the marked appliqué area.

5. Straight-stitch around the marked line for the needlelace inside each appliqué. Cut away the layers close to the stitching, taking care not to cut the stitches. To prevent stretching and distortion, cut only a few sections at a time, make the needlelace, then cut a few more and continue.

6. Following the directions for "Needlelace-in-Appliqué" on pages 45–48, make the lace inside each opening. Use matching thread on the top spool and in the bobbin for the satin stitching as well as the lace.

7. To finish, use a straight stitch and machine stitch close to the outer edges of the appliqués through all layers. Trim the excess fabric close to the stitches, taking care not to cut the stitches.

8. Because the quilt layers are bulky, the edges often ripple when satin-stitched. To prevent this, set the machine for a long basting stitch and stitch over the first row of stitching (step 7), using regular sewing thread for the top spool and bobbin. Start and stop stitching every 2", leaving a thread tail at the beginning and end of each section.

Working from both ends of each section, pull the bobbin thread to draw up the stitching, easing just enough so the edge lies flat all the way around the quilt.

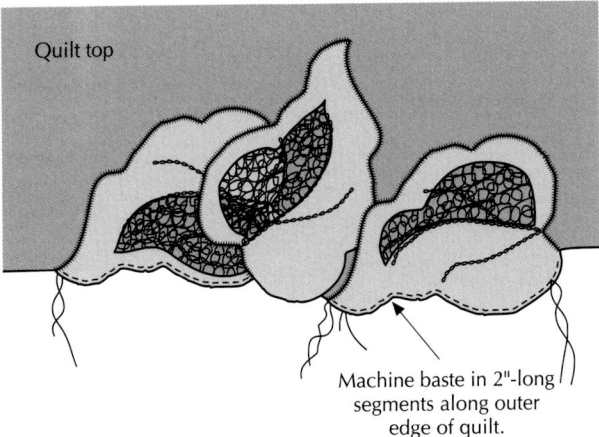

Quilt top

Machine baste in 2"-long segments along outer edge of quilt.

9. Following step 8 in "Stitching the Border" on page 58, complete the quilt border.

SEW CLEVER

When working with the multiple layers in a quilt border, it is not unusual for little bits of thread and batting to poke out after the satin stitching is completed. Use appliqué scissors to trim these away. To disguise stubborn bits, color them, using a permanent magic marker or heat-set silk paint, such as Deka, in a color that matches your thread. The bits won't go away, but they'll blend into the appliqué and won't be as noticeable.

Chapter 8

Creative Variations

Jungle Fever

The tapestry fabric used for the vest and hat of this ensemble was the design inspiration for the embellishments on the jacket. Subtle needlelace worked in the silk linen enhances a fluffy-maned zebra peering from jungle foliage. Computerized decorative stitches enhance the lattice strips that unify the jacket design. The vest underneath was embellished with bobbin couching.

After you've conquered the basics, you might like to try some exciting variations. Take some time now to make samples of these for future reference. It's always easier to incorporate something new into a project if you've tried it at least once and worked out the kinks.

Twin-Needle Stitching

Twin-needle stitching creates denser needlelace. Use a different thread in each needle for wonderful effects. (Refer to the box on page 66 for threading information.) Choose threads in colors and types that complement without overpowering each other. For a lacier effect, sew larger circles. In the holiday napkin shown at right, I used red Sliver thread in one needle, green rayon embroidery thread in the other, and transparent thread in the bobbin.

The wire lace leaves shown below also illustrate the effects of varying the thread types and colors. The red leaves were made using red rayon thread in both needles with purple metallic thread in the bobbin. For the green leaf, I used two different values of green rayon thread in a single, size 18 needle and gold Sliver in the bobbin. The resulting lace looks heavier and resembles crochet.

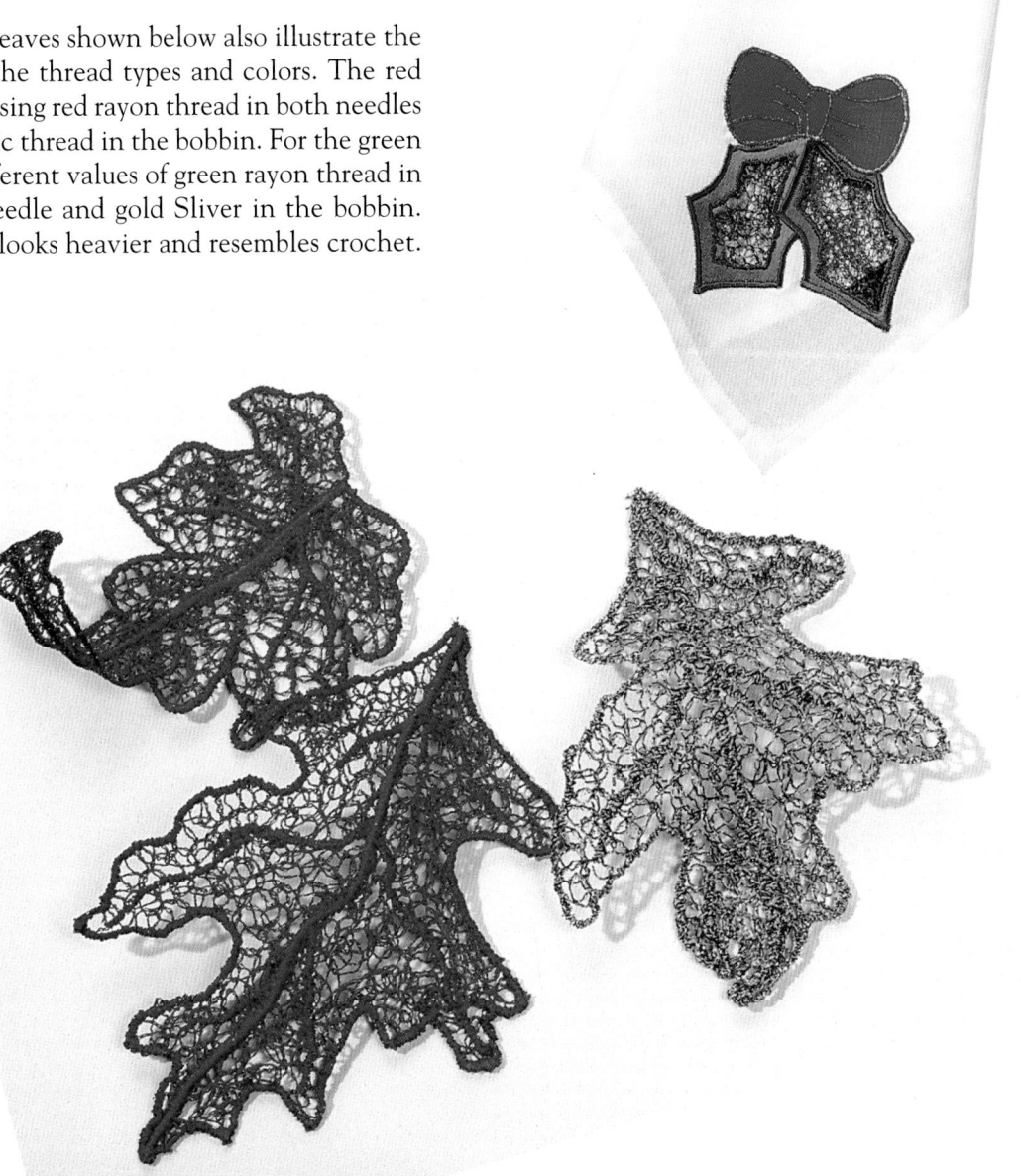

THREADING A TWIN NEEDLE

Twin needles are available in a number of widths (the distance between the two needles, point to point), but I favor the 3mm size. Insert the common shank into the machine as you would any other needle, then thread the machine in the following manner.

Place a spool of thread on each of the two spool pins on your machine, making sure one thread unwinds from the front of the spool and the other from the back. Thread the two threads as one with the following exceptions:

❧ When you reach the tension discs, make sure the threads are on each side of a disc instead of threading both between the discs. On older machines, run the thread through different sides of the circular discs. Each thread should have its own tension if possible. Check your owner's manual for specific instructions.

❧ When threading through the thread guide just above the needle, thread one thread through and leave one free. If your machine has guides for two threads, thread each through the guides, following your owner's-manual instructions.

Thread in front of thread guide →   ← Thread in back of thread guide

❧ Thread the right needle with thread from the right-hand spool, and the left needle with thread from the left-hand spool.

Note

When creating needlelace, you use straight and zigzag stitching. Twin needles will probably hit the darning foot while zigzag stitching. For that reason, switch to a single needle for the zigzag stitch.

~

Needlelace Overlays

Needlelace overlays add dimension to the surface of fiber art. Fiber artist Sue Vernon used circular-stitched lace overlays to create delicate detailing in her quilt shown on page 67. Patsy Eckman made more open lace to embellish the print in her vest on the same page. Directions for both variations are included below.

Circular-Stitched Lace Overlays

1. Set the machine for free-motion straight stitching as directed on pages 40–41.
2. Decide where you want the lace. Use a fine-tip, permanent black marker and trace the desired shape onto a piece of water-soluble stabilizer.
3. Thread the machine. If desired, use a contrasting thread in the bobbin to achieve a two-tone effect.
4. Following the basic directions for "Needlelace-in-Appliqué" on pages 45–48, secure the stabilizer in a spring hoop and make needlelace. *Do not satin- or straight-stitch around the outer edge of the lace.*

5. Trim away the excess stabilizer and dissolve the remainder under gently running tap water. (First, be sure to read the manufacturer's directions for removing the stabilizer.) Allow the lace to dry.
6. Thread a hand-sewing needle with the same thread used to make the lace. Place the lace over the chosen area and tack it in place.

Openwork Lace Overlays

1. Adjust the machine for free-motion straight stitching as described on pages 40–41. Thread the machine with decorative thread on top and your choice of thread in the bobbin: decorative, all-purpose, or transparent thread.
2. Cut 2 pieces of water-soluble stabilizer large enough for the desired overlay shape and place them between 2 pressing cloths. Press with a warm iron to help stiffen the stabilizer. (This method requires more stitching, which would weaken and tear a single layer of stabilizer.)
3. Place the stabilizer in a spring hoop and use a permanent fine-tip black marker to trace the desired shape onto the stabilizer. Draw inside the shape, creating a web of straight lines.
4. Free-motion straight-stitch over every line 2 or 3 times. Don't strive for perfection. You will cover this stitching with zigzag stitching later. You can't zigzag in air (which is really what you're doing when you use a stabilizer); you need the straight-stitched bars as a foundation.

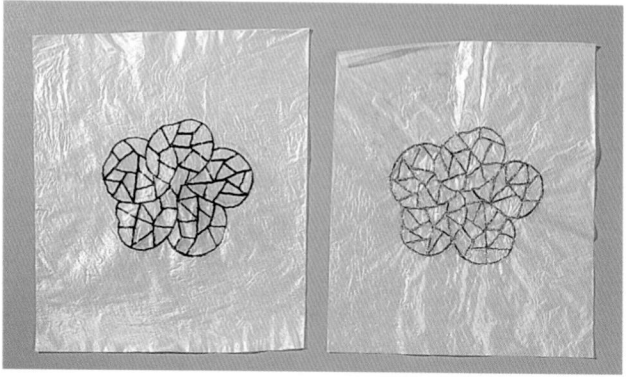

5. Adjust the machine for free-motion zigzag stitching and stitch over the straight-stitched lines, encasing them in thread and making sure all lines are connected to each other. Due to the amount of stitching, don't be surprised if the stabilizer eventually rips. That's OK as long as the design remains intact and the threads don't tangle. If you run into stitching problems because of torn stabilizer, cut a small piece of stabilizer, wet the corners, and stick it in place on the underside of the torn area.
6. Trim away excess stabilizer and dissolve the remainder under gently running tap water. Allow the lace to dry, then sew it in place as described in step 6 of "Circular-Stitched Lace Overlays" on page 66.

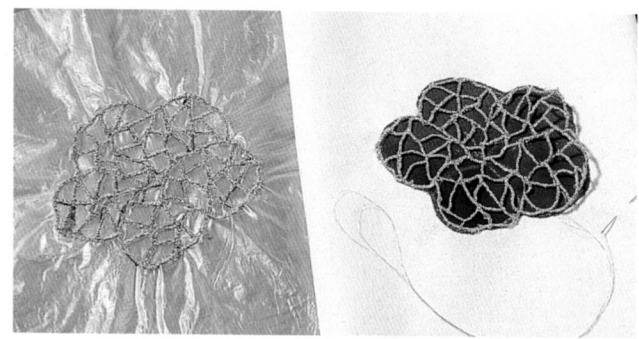

Needlelace Insets in Printed Fabrics

Have fun adding unexpected texture to printed fabrics like the wool challis shown below. Placed randomly in selected areas of the print, needlelace is a subtle accent that invites the viewer to examine the garment more closely. Choose a large overall print for this technique.

1. Cut out the garment pieces and choose an area for needlelace. For added body, back the embellished pieces with a lightweight fusible interfacing. Lay the garment piece, right side up, over a piece of heat-disintegrating stabilizer. Pin throughout.
2. Study the fabric to determine possible areas for embellishment. Leave key areas of the print intact; remove less interesting areas, such as the background. Mark areas with chalk as shown in the photo below.
3. Adjust the machine for free-motion straight stitching as directed on pages 40–41. Thread the needle with decorative thread; use matching sewing thread in the bobbin. You can use any thread color as long as it enhances the fabric.
4. Stitch on the marked line. Trim only the fabric inside and ⅛" away from the stitching, leaving the stabilizer intact.
5. Referring to "Needlelace without Appliqué" on pages 49–50, make needlelace, connecting the stitching to the cut edges of the opening.
6. Finish the raw edges in one of the following ways. If the fabric is heavy or has been backed with fusible interfacing, free-motion satin-stitch over the raw edges. Or, treat the raw edges with a seam sealant, then bobbin-couch a heavier thread to cover the raw edges. (See "Bobbin Couching" on pages 86–87.)
7. Following the manufacturer's instructions, trim away the excess stabilizer and disintegrate the remainder with a hot iron.

Shaded Lace

Using threads of different colors and values, this beautiful variation creates a very dense lace. The resulting needlelace is quite realistic. Monica Anderton, one of my students and an outstanding fiber artist, used this technique to create exceptional color movement in the appliqués on a jacket (shown below). She started with hand-painted appliqué fabric and wanted the lace to continue the effect throughout. Her beautiful interpretation was my inspiration to experiment and develop the technique further.

Create shaded lace inside an appliqué as Monica did by following the steps for "Needlelace-in-Appliqué" on pages 45–49. You will need threads in every color that touches the appliqué opening. Make the lace, changing thread colors when necessary to create gently meandering lines of color.

Consider creating shaded lace without an appliqué. You use the same basic procedure as with an appliqué, but you have more freedom in thread choices.

To create shaded needlelace without an appliqué:

1. Find a colored picture of something you wish to duplicate, and stylize the shape as necessary to make it workable in fiber. Make a template of the shape.
2. Trace around the template on fabric, but do not include any detail lines. Follow steps 5 and 6 of "Needlelace without Appliqué" on pages 49–50 to

prepare the opening for the lace. Using small embroidery scissors, trim the fabric inside and 1/16" from the stitched line. Do not cut the stitching or the stabilizer. You should have an opening in the fabric with the stabilizer still attached.

3. Place the stabilized opening over the picture and divide into areas of color. If you are using heat-

disintegrating stabilizer, color the areas with colored pencils. If you are using water-soluble stabilizer, mark the lines where different color areas begin and end with a permanent marking pen.

4. Use the picture as a reference while you stitch the needlelace. Use a variety of decorative threads compatible with the stabilizer you are using and in the appropriate colors to duplicate the design. (Use transparent thread in the bobbin if using water-soluble stabilizer. Use high-heat-tolerant thread in the bobbin if using heat-disintegrating stabilizer.)

Stitch *small*, overlapping circles to create a dense lace, changing thread colors as necessary to match the color areas in the design. Avoid abrupt color changes. To end one color, stop at any point and cut the thread flush with the stabilizer. Start the next color where the first color ended.

5. Finish the outer edge of the lace with free-motion satin stitching, using the most dominant color in the shaded lace. Following the manufacturer's instructions, dissolve or disintegrate the stabilizer.

Embroidered and Appliquéd Lace

Here's another exciting way to embellish your work and use the machine creatively. Make a needlelace inset, then add machine-embroidered and appliquéd embellishments. This beautiful variation can be used in many areas of garment construction. Because the lace background is very soft, it works best where a soft drape is required. Sleeve edges as well as skirt, dress, vest, and tunic hems are ideal for this treatment, but you can also use it for insets as shown in the photo at right.

You can create the effect of embroidered lace with thread and additional appliqué pieces. The lace backdrop for the cranberry velveteen vest shown in progress on the following pages was created with cranberry rayon embroidery thread on the top spool and gold metallic thread in the bobbin.

The threads discussed on pages 19–20 are appropriate for this type of lacework, and each contributes its own unique look. Keep in mind that the lace backdrop should have a subtle quality to show off the embroidery or appliqué on top. Burmilana and #30 rayon are dense threads, making them ideal for embroidering on top of needlelace made with finer threads. Metallic, #40 rayon, and #50 silk are also good possibilities. Of course, the thread you use should be compatible in color and texture with the fashion fabric you have chosen.

When making embroidered lace, choose an area for insertion and complete the lace inset before completing any of the garment construction. A vest pattern is used for the steps that follow.

1. Choose an area where you would like to add lace in place of the fashion fabric. Sketch it in and hold the pattern up to yourself in front of a mirror to make sure you like the size and placement. Avoid placing the inset so it draws attention where you don't want it. Copy the pattern piece on paper or tracing cloth, transferring all notches and construction symbols.

2. Mark the copy where the top of the lace inset is to begin. It helps to use the alteration lines that are preprinted on the pattern as a guide for positioning straight cutting lines. Draw the top line of your inset parallel to the alteration line, then measure down the desired width and draw the bottom line. Take into account any pleats, darts, or other construction features, making sure the inset clears these areas.

3. For easier matching during construction, use a colored pencil (in a color different than the previous lines) to draw a line perpendicular to the 2 marked lines. Cut the pattern apart on the 2 marked lines, making 3 pieces: the upper front, the lower front, and the lace inset.

4. Add a ⅝"-wide seam allowance to each cut edge as shown in the photo.

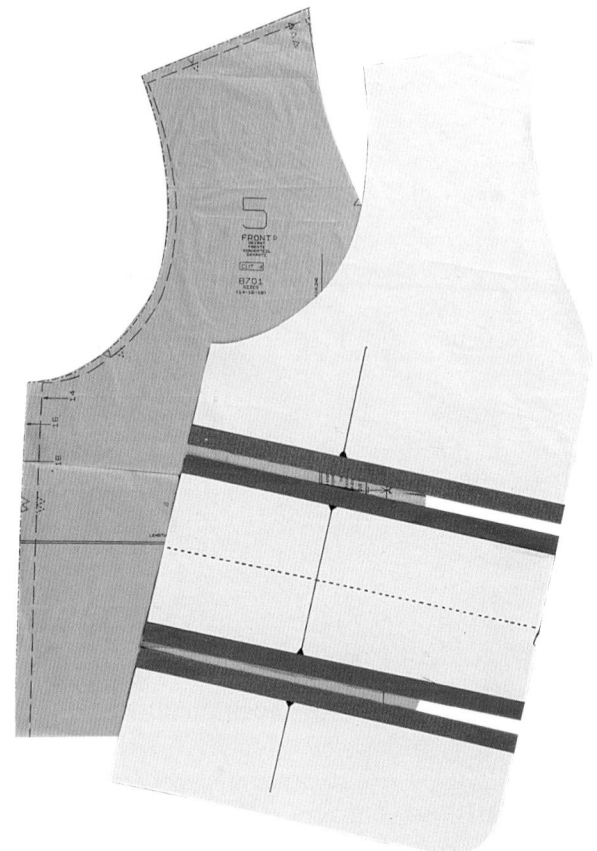

5. Set the inset pattern piece aside for now and cut all the other garment pieces from the fashion fabric, including the adjusted upper and lower front pattern pieces. Remember to observe grain lines. When cutting, add a notch or an ⅛"-deep clip to indicate the position of the line you drew in step 3.

6. Choose an embroidery design. The design elements don't need to connect, but they should clear the seam allowances unless you intend for them to extend into the fashion fabric. This continuation of the design

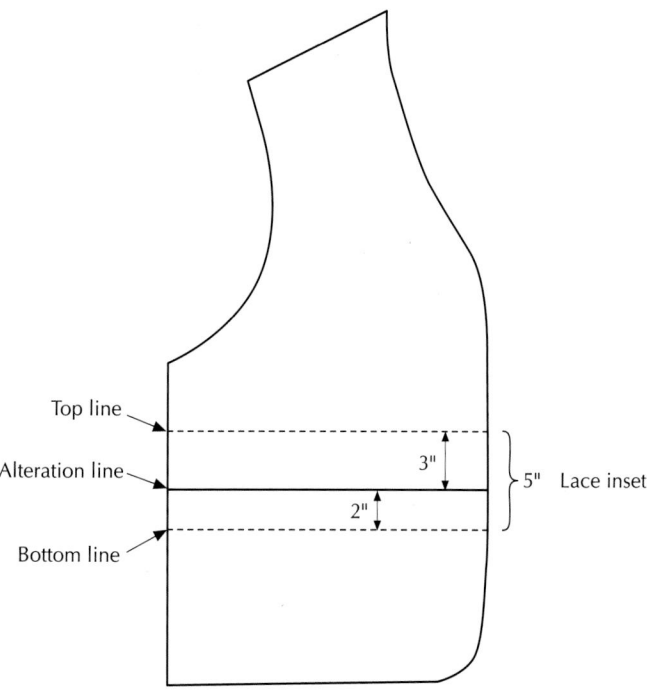

Top line

Alteration line

Bottom line

3"

2"

} 5" Lace inset

can be very interesting, especially when just a few elements are extended beyond the needlelace.

DESIGNING WITH EASE

I find the easiest approach to designing in this area is to play with paper designs on top of the paper pattern. Another effective way is to make a second inset pattern piece out of tracing paper and place it over design shapes so you can see what fits.

7. Choose a stabilizer according to design needs. Remember, some threads are heat sensitive and can't be used with heat-disintegrating stabilizers. I prefer heat-disintegrating stabilizer when sewing large areas of embroidered lace. It is strong and holds its shape better than water-soluble stabilizer. It's also very dense and doesn't require a hoop. For small areas of lace, you may prefer water-soluble stabilizer. If so, use a double layer in a spring hoop.

Lay the piece of stabilizer over the pattern piece for the inset. The stabilizer is several inches larger than the pattern and must fit into the hoop if you are using one. Use a fine-tip, permanent black marker to trace the pattern. Mark all notches and seam lines.

Trace the embroidery design onto the stabilizer, including all detail lines. Use a fine black marker so you can see the design through the lace backdrop.

The part of the design that extends into the fabric area will be stitched later. However, I recommend tracing the entire design since it serves as a reference point.

8. Set the machine for free-motion straight stitching as directed on pages 40–41. Thread the needle and bobbin with decorative thread. The threads don't have to be the same color, but the difference should be subtle enough so it doesn't compete with the embroidery. Make a very dense needlelace to cover the entire inset pattern piece. (See "Needlelace Basics" on pages 43–50.)

9. Thread the machine for embroidery. It's great fun to watch the lace take on a whole new personality as you add the embroidery. For a refined look, use the same thread you used for the lace. As an option, use the same color but in a thread of a different type or texture—red metallic embroidery on top of red rayon lace, for example. For drama, use a contrasting thread. If adding appliqués, see "Appliqué Variation" below.

Set the machine for a zigzag stitch and outline the design shapes with a free-motion satin stitch. Use a wide satin stitch to create heavier lines.

Now is the time to call on your creativity. Outline the design only, or outline first and then fill the entire design motif with thread. Or, outline and then add some detail lines. Use fabric appliqués in some of the design areas, or try using several different threads. It's your choice.

Stitch the designs up to the seam lines. Anything beyond that will not be seen since you would be stitching in the seam allowances. If you want the design to extend into the fashion fabric, do that after you have joined the lace inset to the garment pieces.

10. Cut out the completed lace inset on the cutting lines. Set the machine for normal sewing, and thread the machine with all-purpose thread to match the fashion fabric.

11. Pin the inset to the garment pieces, right sides together, with notches and matching clips or notches aligned. Stitch the seams, then press them toward the fabric.

12. To secure the seam allowances, topstitch through all layers of the vest fabric and lace inset, close to each seam line.

13. To complete any embroidery or appliqué that extends into the fabric, position the original design pattern over the garment and line up the design shapes. Using dressmaker's carbon or chalk paper, transfer unstitched areas of the design onto the fabric. Free-motion zigzag stitch on the marked designs.

14. Following the manufacturer's directions, remove the stabilizer.

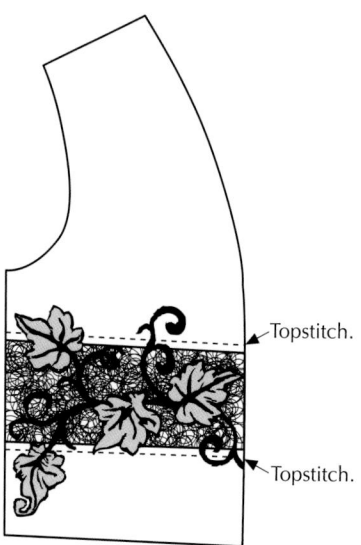

Topstitch.

Topstitch.

APPLIQUÉ VARIATION

You can use appliqués as well as embroidery for the lace insets. Consider extending appliqués onto the fashion fabric, over the seam lines, for a more interesting look.

1. Make templates of the embroidery design and trace the shapes onto appliqué fabric fused to paper-backed fusible web.

2. Cut out the appliqué shapes, remove the paper backing, and position them on the lace inset, using the paper pattern as a guide.

3. Machine appliqué, using traditional satin stitching as described on page 38. Satin-stitch all detail lines.

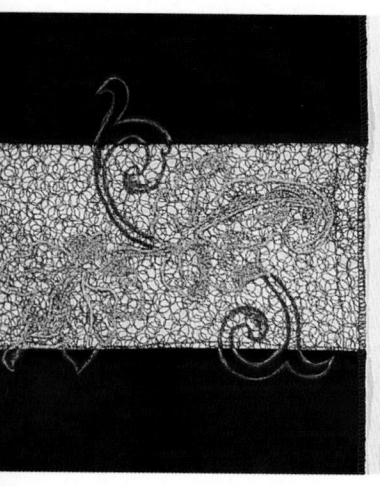
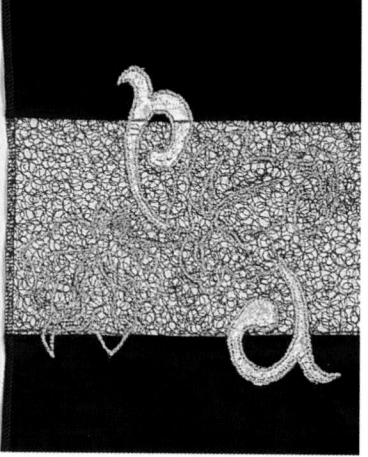

Chapter 9

Dimensional Embellishments

Tiger Lily Princess in the Land of Painted Dreams

Three-dimensional, hand-painted tiger lilies grace the straps and asymmetrical dropped waistline of this enchanting evening dress. Beading outlines the wired edges of each petal. Lightweight wire encased in stitching makes it possible to shape each petal for a more realistic effect. Photo by Brad Stanton.

*F*iber art is exciting and much more interesting when dimension is added. Flowers, leaves, butterfly wings, even abstract geometrics—these and many other shapes can be made into dimensional forms. This chapter leads you through the steps required to create intriguing dimensional shapes and will inspire you with other ideas for creating dimension.

To create three-dimensional needlelace shapes, use a free-motion sewing setup with your choice of threads. You can create the shapes from lightweight fabric too. To begin, choose a design shape with simple lines. More intricate designs work for the one-dimensional appliqués that lie beneath dimensional shapes. If necessary, stylize the shape as described on page 27. Then choose from the construction methods described in this chapter.

Cattleyan Rhapsody

Made from hand-dyed and hand-painted fabrics, this ensemble was designed for the 1989–90 Fairfield Fashion Show. Orchids of hand-painted silk noil were appliquéd with rayon and metallic embroidery threads. Some orchids have free-standing petals, adding eye-catching three-dimensional interest. Photo by Brad Stanton.

"Butterflies are Free" is my original design. Hand-dyed fabrics were embellished with machine embroidery, thread fuzzies, bobbin work, and dimensional dragonflies.

Petals

Three-dimensional work is realistic when you combine it with one-dimensional appliqué. The poppy at left is an excellent example. Some of the petals were appliquéd to the background fabric, while the remaining petals were constructed using dimensional techniques.

Method One
Materials

Flower pattern on page 95 or use your own design.
9" x 22" solid-color fabric for flower
9" x 22" piece of paper-backed fusible web
9" x 22" piece of iron-on, tear-away stabilizer
Decorative thread to match fabric
3 pieces of #32-gauge wire, each 12" long
¼ yd. water-soluble stabilizer
7"-diameter spring embroidery hoop
Fabric marking pen

Note
Adapt these directions to make the iris, using the pattern on page 93.

Directions

1. Thread the needle and bobbin with thread to match the fabric. Cut the flower fabric into 2 equal pieces and apply fusible web to the wrong side of 1 piece.
2. Use a fabric marker to trace the base pattern onto the right side of the web-backed fabric. The flower shown has a total of 8 petals. Five were appliquéd, and 3 more were made for dimensional shaping. Cut out the base appliqués, remove the backing paper, position on the background, and fuse in place.
3. Apply the tear-away stabilizer to the wrong side of the background fabric, under the appliqué.
4. Machine appliqué, using your choice of the methods discussed in Chapter 4. Add any detail lines you wish to the base appliqué piece. Remove the stabilizer.

5. Trace the remaining petals onto the remaining web-backed fabric. Cut on the marked line. These are the tops of the three petals. Remove the paper backing and arrange the petals right side up on the wrong side of the remaining flower fabric. Leaving at least ½" around each petal, fuse in place.

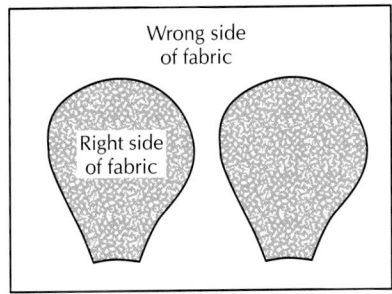

Wrong side of fabric

Right side of fabric

6. Lay a piece of #32-gauge wire along the edge of each petal, leaving a 1"-long tail at each end. Leave the bottom open as shown. Set the machine for a long, narrow zigzag stitch; couch the wire in place. The wire will show through the stitching.

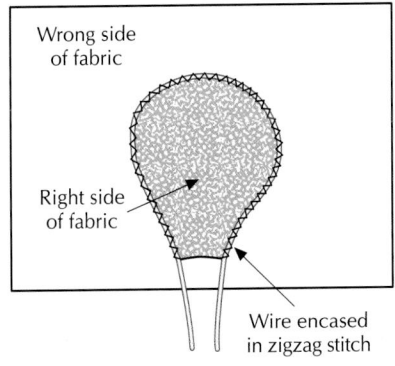

Wrong side of fabric

Right side of fabric

Wire encased in zigzag stitch

7. Cut out the petal as close to the stitching as possible without cutting the stitches.
8. Secure a piece of water-soluble stabilizer in the spring hoop. Pin the wired petal on top of the stabilizer. Free-motion satin-stitch around the edge to enclose and cover the wire. Trim the stabilizer and dissolve any remaining pieces with water.

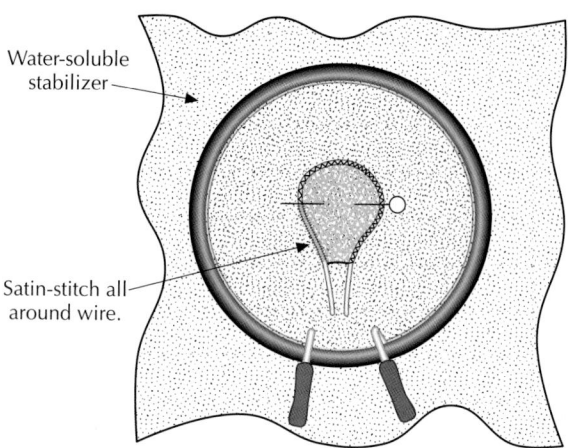

Water-soluble stabilizer

Satin-stitch all around wire.

9. Use wire cutters or old scissors to trim the excess wire. Pinch the straight end to make a pleat and stitch to the center of the appliquéd flower. Repeat with the remaining wired petals. Stagger the petals to fall in between the base petals for a more pleasing effect.

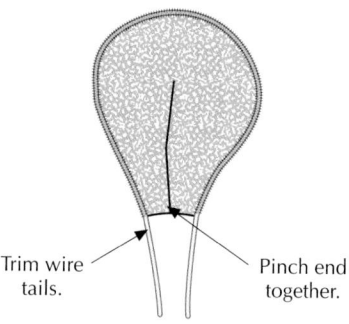

Trim wire tails.

Pinch end together.

10. Cover the raw edges of the petals with a "thread fuzzy" (page 82) or beads (page 83).

Method Two

This method makes it easier to sew petals or any small shape. Refer to the Materials list for Method One on page 77. However, you will not need fusible web or stabilizer for this method.

1. Trace around the petals on the wrong side of a large piece of flower fabric. Place this piece on top of a second piece of fabric, right sides together, and straight-stitch around each petal shape on the marked lines, leaving the bottom open for turning.
2. Cut out each petal ⅛" from the stitching and turn right side out.

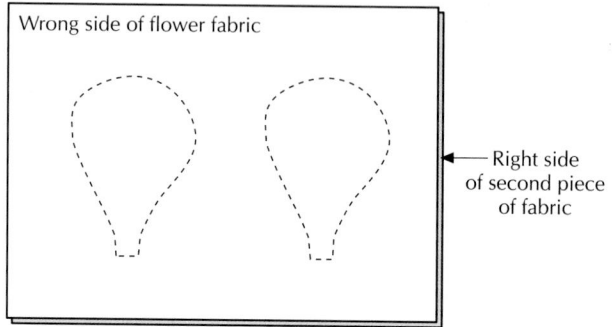

Wrong side of flower fabric

Right side of second piece of fabric

Trace petal design on wrong side of fabric. Stitch on traced lines.

3. Position a piece of #32-gauge wire through the center of the petal—like a vein—extending it 2" beyond each end. Using a decorative thread that matches the fabric, satin-stitch over the wire. Gently gather the fabric along the wire. Trim the excess wire at each end with wire cutters or old scissors. Flatten the petal to remove the gathers; the ends of the wire will disappear under the stitching.
4. Pleat the bottom (unfinished edge) of the petal, and tack to the base fabric by hand or machine.

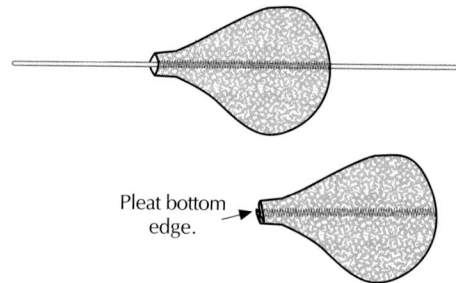

Pleat bottom edge.

5. Cover the raw edges of the petals with a thread fuzzy (page 82) or beads (pages 83).

Method Three

Nonwoven fabrics are wonderful for dimensional work because the cut edges are already finished. Doubling the fabric gives the shape substantial body. Synthetic suede and felt work well with this method.

Materials

Scraps of synthetic suede or felt
Rayon machine-embroidery thread to match fabric
7"-diameter spring embroidery hoop
3 pieces of #32-gauge wire, each 12" long

Directions

1. Pin 2 pieces of suede or felt wrong sides together. (Use fine silk pins on synthetic suede.) Using a fabric marker, trace the desired number of petals on one side of the layered fabric.
2. Using matching all-purpose thread, machine straight-stitch just inside the marked lines.
3. Without cutting out the petals yet, follow step 3 of Method Two on page 78.
4. Cut out each petal a little beyond the stitched line, removing the markings if necessary. Pleat the petal as directed in step 4 of Method Two. Attach to the background and finish with a thread fuzzy or beads.

Insects

Freestanding insects, such as dragonflies and butterflies, made entirely of thread are one of my favorite dimensional effects. Patterns for both appear on page 91.

Materials

¼ yd. water-soluble stabilizer
Fine-tip permanent marker
7"-diameter spring embroidery hoop
Metallic machine-embroidery thread
3 pieces of #32-gauge wire, each 12" long

Directions

1. Using a permanent marker, trace each wing onto water-soluble stabilizer. Leave ½" to 1" between each wing for attaching the wire. Place the marked stabilizer in the spring hoop.
2. Adjust the machine for free-motion stitching, and use decorative thread for the top spool and bobbin. Both sides of the work will show, so the threads must be compatible.
3. Referring to "Needlelace without Appliqué" on pages 49–50, create needlelace inside the marked wing area.

4. To attach wire to the wings, set your machine for free-motion zigzag stitching. Place the wire along the edge of the wing shape and encase it in satin stitching, making sure that it connects to the lace. Trim the wire tails to ½". Gently remove the excess stabilizer and dissolve any remaining bits.

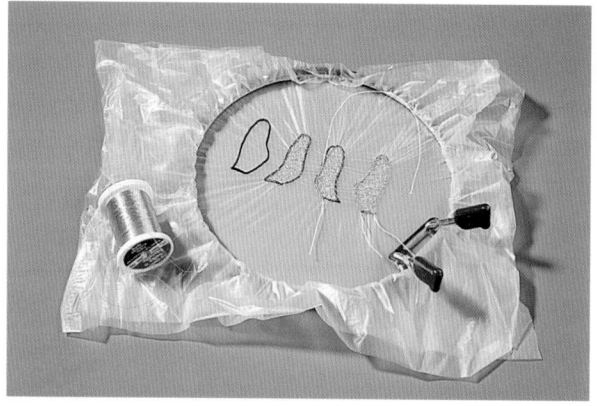

5. Using a fine-tip permanent marker, trace the body pattern onto a piece of water-soluble stabilizer. Center the body in the hoop. Use a free-motion straight stitch to outline the body shape.
6. Attach the wings while the body is still in the hoop. Position them where you want them, laying the wire ends inside the body outline. Stitch over the wire ends to hold the wings in place, then fill the body with free-motion zigzag or straight stitching to cover the outline stitching and wire ends.

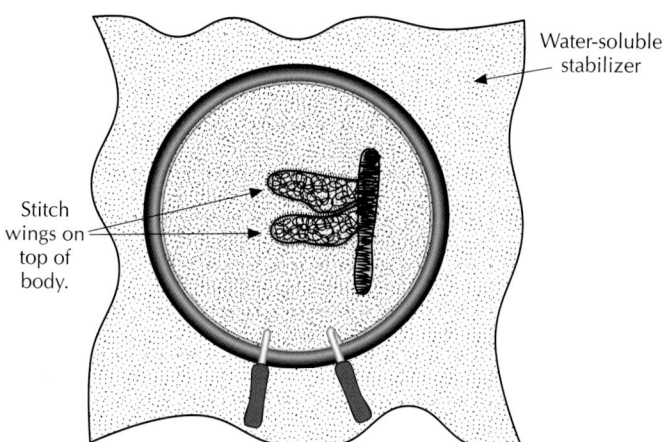

Water-soluble stabilizer

Stitch wings on top of body.

7. Trim excess stabilizer from around the body and dissolve any remaining stabilizer. Tack the dragonfly to the background. Tack only enough to hold the piece securely to keep it as free as possible. For a removable piece, attach a jewelry-pin back to the underside.
8. To make antennae, satin-stitch over wire laid on a piece of stabilizer. Attach to the head as described for the wings.

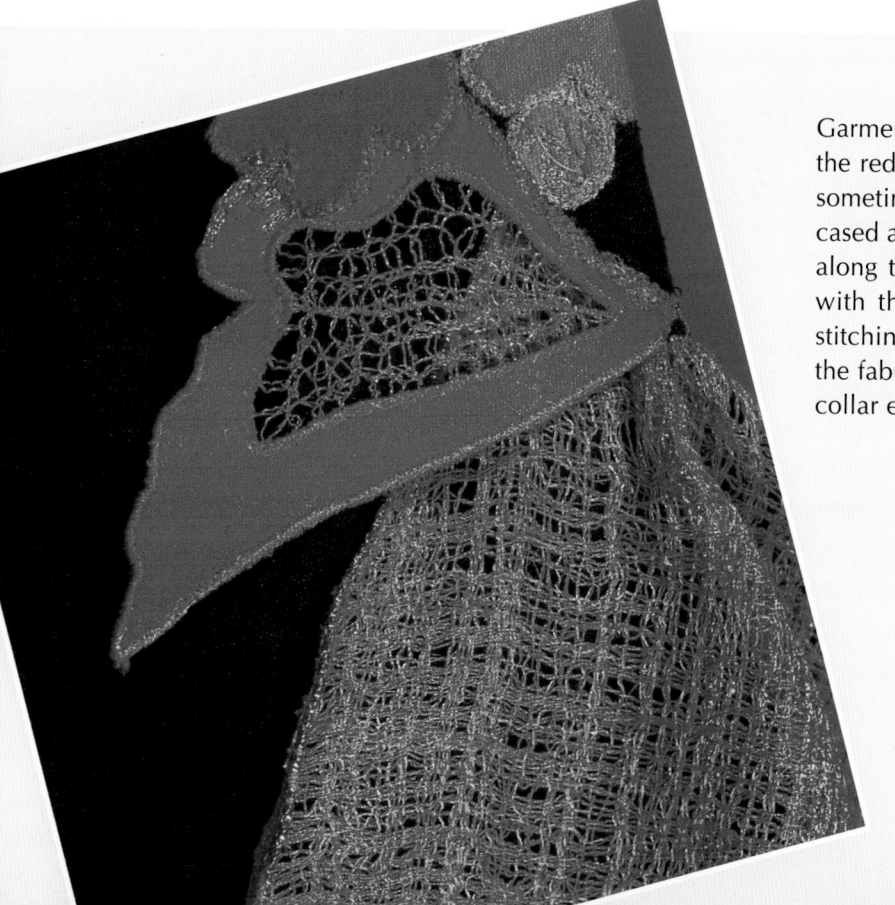

GET WIRED!

Garment areas with heavy machine work, such as the red lace collar on the jacket shown at left, can sometimes curl. To keep the collar lying flat, I encased a piece of #32-gauge wire with satin stitching along the outer edge of the collar. For best results with this technique, gather the fabric a bit after stitching the wire, then trim the wire and smooth out the fabric to hide the ends. You can then shape the collar edge as desired so it lies against the garment.

Thread-Covered Wire

You'll be amazed at the uses you'll find for thread-covered wire in wearables, on quilts, and for home-decorating projects.

Materials

#18-gauge wire and wire cutters
Heavy thread and textured yarn, such as mohair, bouclé, or chenille
Craft paste
Pencil or knitting needle

Directions

1. Cover a straight piece of wire with paste.
2. Hold the paste-coated wire in one hand and yarn in the other. Attach the yarn to one end of the wire and turn the wire slowly so the yarn winds itself around the wire and covers it.
3. Allow the paste to dry completely, then curl the wrapped wire around a pencil or knitting needle. Pull the curled wire from the pencil and shape the curls as desired.

Thread Fuzzies

Round thread fuzzies, otherwise known as pompons, make exotic centers for dimensional flowers or hold their own as flowers. Elongated fuzzies look like caterpillars crawling on a branch or the mane of a jungle animal.

You can make thread fuzzies in a variety of sizes, using heavy thread or yarn. Trim the cut ends for a neat look or leave them untrimmed for a more natural look. Creating a thread fuzzy takes just a few minutes and a minimal amount of materials. The technique is similar to making a pompon.

To make a round fuzzy:

1. Wind 1 yard of couching yarn around the center of a 2" square of cardboard. Use more or less yarn, depending on how full you want the fuzzy.
2. Carefully remove the thread bundle from the cardboard and twist it in the center to make a figure eight. Place it in its permanent position on the garment or quilt and stitch across the center to secure. (Use a very short straight stitch and be careful to catch all the threads.)
3. Cut the looped ends of the bundle and use a small wire brush (from the paint department in a home-improvement or hardware store) to fray the ends. Trim the ends or leave as is.

Wrap.   Twist and stitch.

← Cut.

To make an elongated fuzzy:

1. Cut and bend a heavy wire (such as a coat hanger) into a long U shape. The distance between each side of the U should be 1½".
2. Beginning at the open end of the U, wrap the yarn around the wire. Work from the open end to the loop end. When finished wrapping, leave the excess yarn attached. (Put the ball of yarn or thread in your lap.)
3. Place the yarn-wrapped wire under the all-purpose presser foot on your sewing machine, with the closed end of the U closest to you. Straight-stitch through the center, parallel to the legs of the U, for 1" or more. As necessary, pull the stitched yarn off the open end of the U and wrap more yarn over the closed end of the U while it is still on the sewing machine. This way, you can make a fringe fuzzy as long as you need.
4. Position the completed fuzzy on the background or machine stitch through the center over the first stitching. Cut the loops and fray with a wire brush, or leave as is.

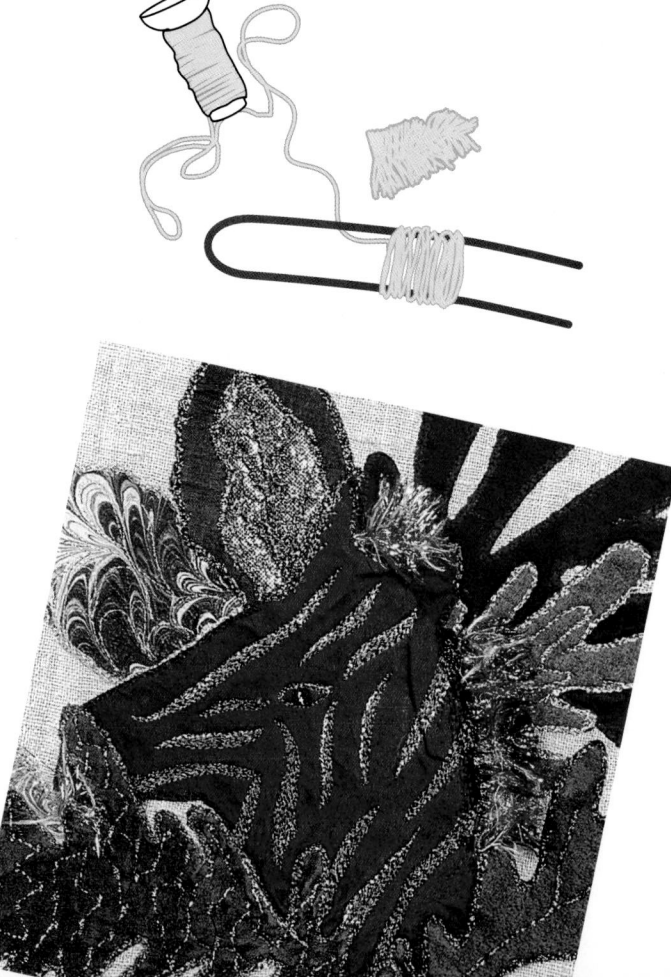

Beads

In the course of my travels, I buy beads wherever I can, knowing that eventually they will find a home in my fiber art. I enjoy just taking them out to play with from time to time—just as I love to play with favorite fabrics from my collection.

A varied selection of beads on hand offers plenty of design inspiration. If you have not yet begun to collect them, start at your local crafts stores and check the phone book for bead stores, especially when visiting large metropolitan areas.

Tiny seed beads are available in a wide range of colors and finishes, including crystal, metallic, and opaque. Scatter them in completed lace, or cluster them in flower centers as fiber artist Marjorie McDonald did on her vest (above right). They make great animal eyes too.

Bugle beads are longer than seed beads, ranging from $1/4$" to 1" in length. I used them at the center of the dimensional tiger lily in one of my Fairfield Fashion Show garments, shown at right. (See also page 75.)

Chapter 10

Bobbin Work

*D*ecorative threads that are too heavy for the needle can be applied to the right side of the fabric by winding them onto the bobbin and then stitching from the wrong side. You can use this method to make bobbin lace and to bobbin-couch thicker threads and yarns. To prepare your bobbin for any of these techniques, see "Preparing the Bobbin" at right.

PREPARING THE BOBBIN

When using heavier threads in the bobbin, you will probably find it necessary to loosen the tension. A tiny screw controls the bobbin tension spring. Turning it counterclockwise loosens it; turning it clockwise tightens it. If your machine doesn't have a removable bobbin case, the screw is usually inside the bobbin area. Check your owner's manual for details.

Hold the bobbin case over a towel or white paper when adjusting the tension so you can find the tiny tension screw if it falls out. If you are uncomfortable with adjusting the bobbin tension for fear you won't be able to get back to balanced tension for normal sewing, buy a second bobbin case for decorative work. Mark it with red fingernail polish to easily identify it. Some machine models have a special case just for decorative work.

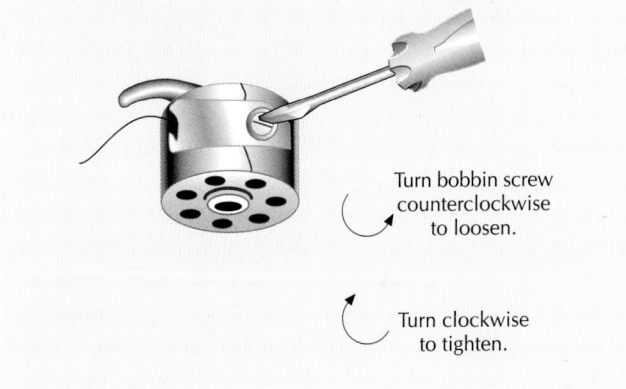

Turn bobbin screw counterclockwise to loosen.

Turn clockwise to tighten.

◄ *The Empress' New Clothes*

Anyone, empress or not, would feel like royalty in this stunning evening ensemble. Hand marbling and then machine quilting the tissue lamé for the jacket required lots of experimentation to "get it right." Hand-painted silk-charmeuse appliqués and machine needlelace provide design interest along the hemline and front slit of the long velvet skirt. Underneath the jacket, a silk organza blouse covers a matching silk charmeuse camisole. The edges of the flounced collar were serged over fishing line to create a fluted edge. Double-piped tissue lamé and charmeuse finish the front, neckline, and sleeve edges of the simply styled jacket. Photo by Brad Stanton.

Bobbin Couching

For years, I have played with unusual threads in the bobbin, adjusting the bobbin tension to my heart's content and sewing on the wrong side of the fabric so the bobbin thread appears on the right side. I didn't know the name for this technique at the time. You may know it as cable stitching; I call it bobbin couching.

Bobbin couching allows you to work with a range of threads and yarns that simply won't fit through the eye of a sewing-machine needle. You can use many of the decorative stitches on your machine for bobbin couching.

I like to use bobbin couching to create positive and negative design areas in my work. This way, the bobbin thread is pronounced in the positive areas, and the fabric pops out in the negative areas. Velveteen and hand-painted silk are two of my favorite fabrics for this method.

Bobbin couching is a versatile technique. A vest pattern is used here to illustrate the process.

1. Choose a simple vest pattern and a simple design motif to surround with couching. The motif can have detail lines, but should have large interior blank areas to show off the fashion fabric.

Design has too many small pieces.

Design with large areas shows fashion fabric.

2. Decide whether or not to use a layer of batting, which adds more depth to the finished work. For a flatter look, don't use batting and ignore all references to batting and backing in the following steps. If adding a layer of batting, you will also need a lightweight backing fabric. I often use nonwoven pattern tracing cloth. Nylon tulle, a finer version of nylon net, is another possibility. You will line the garment later, so the backing will not show in the completed garment.

3. Trim the pattern pieces that will be embellished with bobbin couching. If you are embellishing both vest fronts, cut a second front from tissue paper or tracing cloth so you have a left and right pattern piece. Trace or pin the design motif on the right side of each pattern piece. (The design should be heavily marked.)

4. Place the pattern pieces on the backing fabric, right sides together. Position the pieces as they will hang on your body. (It's important to see how the designs will relate to each other on the finished garment). Use a fine-tip, permanent black marker to trace each pattern piece onto the backing.

5. To transfer the design motifs, slip the pattern pieces underneath the marked areas of the duplicating material, matching the traced line with the edge of the pattern. The pattern is facing down but the design will show through. Trace the design onto the tissue paper or tracing cloth.

6. Place a piece of fashion fabric the same size as the backing right side down on a flat surface and smooth a piece of batting on top. Next, place the backing fabric with tracings right side up on top. Smooth out any wrinkles. Using long straight pins or small safety pins, pin the layers together as shown.

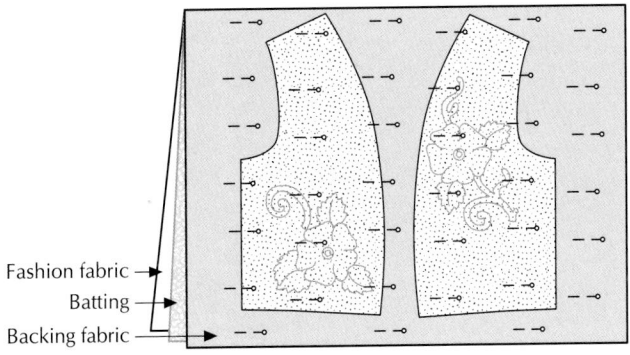

Fashion fabric →
Batting →
Backing fabric →

Use a lot of pins and stagger them; remove those near or in the hoop.

7. Place the layered fabrics in a spring hoop with the backing fabric on top. Adjust the machine for free-motion straight stitching as described on pages 40–41. Wind three or four bobbins full of the selected couching yarn or thread. Thread the needle with matching thread. Adjust the bobbin tension as necessary.

8. Position the hooped fabric under the darning foot at one of the design motifs. Hold the top thread while you turn the handwheel to draw up the bobbin thread. Stitch the motif outline and detail lines. Pull all thread tails to the wrong side, tie off, and trim close to the surface of the work. Stitch around all motifs and detail lines before filling in the blank areas.

9. Adjust the hoop so you can work in an area without any motif. Bring the bobbin thread to the top and stitch in a meandering pattern to fill the blank areas. Notice that no line of stitching crosses or touches another. The lines can be close together or far apart,

but aim for consistency throughout. Bring the thread tails to the back, tie off, and trim close to the surface of the work.

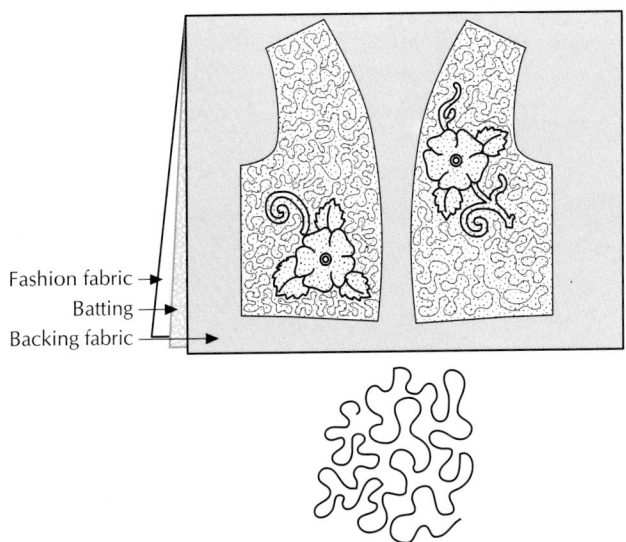

Fashion fabric →
Batting →
Backing fabric →

Meander Stitching

Bobbin couching is not limited to positive and negative work. I use it to accentuate appliqué designs as shown on the sleeve of this black silk noil jacket. I did the appliqué work first, then added the couching.

Stumpwork

This strange-sounding technique is a relative of bobbin couching. Essentially, you bobbin-couch as described above, then go over it again to build up stitches. I use it to frame the center of small quilt tops as shown below, but you can adapt it for other uses.

1. Select a print with fairly large motifs, and cut it to the size of the quilt top. Fuse paper-backed fusible web to the wrong side of this fabric.

2. Using a fine-tip marker or a dark pencil, trace the desired motifs onto the paper backing. Motifs meander and stay connected on the inner edge of a quilt frame, but you can also trace selected single motifs.

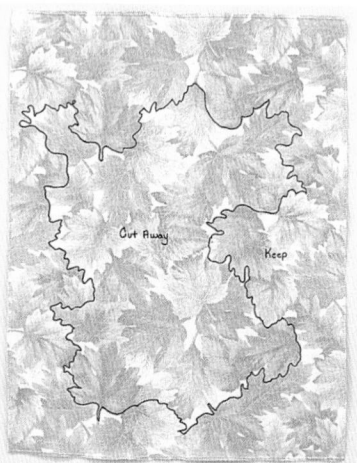

3. Cut away the negative areas, then remove the paper backing from the remaining frame and selected shapes. Position the shapes and frame on the quilt top and pin in place. Examine the composition, make any desired changes, and then fuse. For added interest, trace one or more of the print motifs onto template plastic and cut them out, then position as desired and trace onto the quilt along the inner edge of the frame.

4. Layer the quilt top with batting and backing; baste. Complete any quilting or appliqué in the quilt center before finishing the frame.

Adjust the machine for free-motion straight stitching as described on pages 40–41. Use a thread to match your couching material on top and in the bobbin. Place the layered quilt in a spring hoop, and free-motion straight-stitch around each motif along the inner edge of the frame. If you traced additional motifs inside the appliquéd frame, outline them with free-motion straight stitching too. This marks the position of the pieces on the backing, the side from which you will stitch to do the bobbin couching.

5. Fill a bobbin with your couching thread or yarn and test-stitch. Adjust the bobbin tension as needed. Position the work in the hoop with the backing fabric right

side up so you can see the free-motion straight stitching. Place the hoop under the needle at a stitching line. Hold the top thread and turn the handwheel to bring the bobbin thread to the top. Stitch, stopping every $1/2$" or so to retrace the stitching so the

bobbin thread builds up. It's especially effective in nooks and crannies of the motifs that make up the frame. Draw the thread ends to the back, tie off, and clip close to the surface or bury them in the batting layer.

TIE IT OFF

When you use this technique on quilts, you must bury the thread in the batting. When used in clothing that will be lined, you can simply tie off the threads on the inside. The lining will hide the thread ends.

Machine-Bobbin Lace

You can use couching yarns to create the look of hand-crocheted lace. Make lace on water-soluble stabilizer, using heavy threads such as Candlelight, Pearl Crown Rayon, or Ribbon Floss in the bobbin and *matching thread in the needle*. For example, if you use a metallic yarn in the bobbin, use metallic machine-embroidery thread on top.

Test stitch on stabilizer in a hoop, adjusting the bobbin tension as necessary. Draw the desired shape on water-soluble stabilizer and, referring to "Needlelace Basics" on pages 43–50," make needlelace. You can free-motion straight-stitch randomly, or you can start in the center and work toward the outer edge.

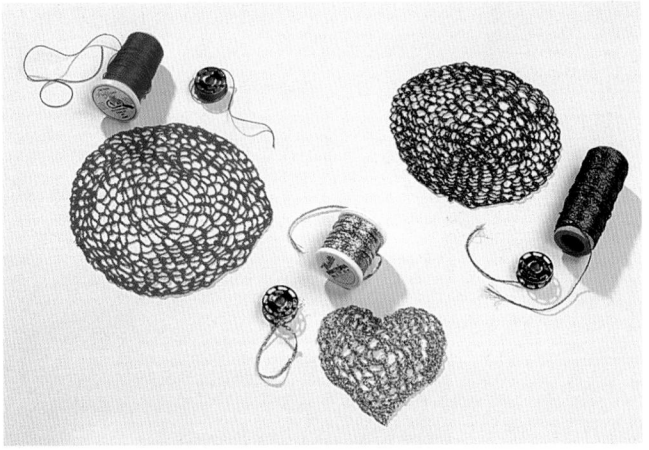

Note
You can make bobbin lace inside an appliqué too, but the detail lines and edge stitching require a different thread setup. Rethread the bobbin with transparent thread or a sewing thread to match the top spool. To stitch the detail lines and edges, turn the work right side up and stitch on top of the lace.

Bobbin Curls

For many years, I was a tole painter and used tendrils as a finishing flourish. I often use tole patterns for clothing embellishment, but now I make tendrils from thread. Because tendrils have many tight configurations, adjust the machine for free-motion stitching.

1. After completing the other embellishments, chalk-mark the desired curls, swirls, and squiggles. I find it's easier to stand over the garment and use my entire arm (not just my wrist and hand) to draw to get the right look. Let the tendrils intertwine in and around other design elements to connect and soften the overall look.
2. To transfer the tendril patterns to the wrong side of your fabric (where you will stitch), place a piece of carbon paper underneath them, with the carbon against the wrong side of the fabric. Run a blunt tapestry needle over the tendrils on the right side to transfer the carbon to the wrong side.

CHALK IT UP!

On dark fabric, dressmaker carbon often doesn't show up. Make your own "white carbon paper" by rubbing white chalk on a piece of paper. Place the chalked side against the wrong side of the fabric, and transfer as with carbon paper.

3. Adjust the machine for free-motion straight stitching. Use transparent thread (or thread that matches the couching yarn) on the top spool. Wind the bobbin with couching yarn or thread that is thin enough to work with some tension. For this method, do not use heavy threads that require no tension.
4. Place the work in a spring hoop, wrong side up. Place the hoop under the needle. Hold the top thread and turn the handwheel to bring the bobbin thread to the top. Holding both threads, take the first stitch. Continue stitching on the marked lines, developing a rhythm as you go and working so the stitches are spaced 8 to 10 per inch. The longer stitch allows the heavy thread to lie smoothly. Shorter stitches will bunch on the right side. Sometimes a tendril extends beyond the hoop opening. Sew until the hoop interferes, then stop with the needle down, and reposition the hoop around the next section of the tendril. Complete the tendril.
5. Bring all thread tails to the wrong side, tie off, and clip, leaving a short tail.

SEW SMART

To couch along the edge of a piece of needlelace where it connects to fabric, turn the piece to the wrong side and stitch around the lace, following the first line of stitching.

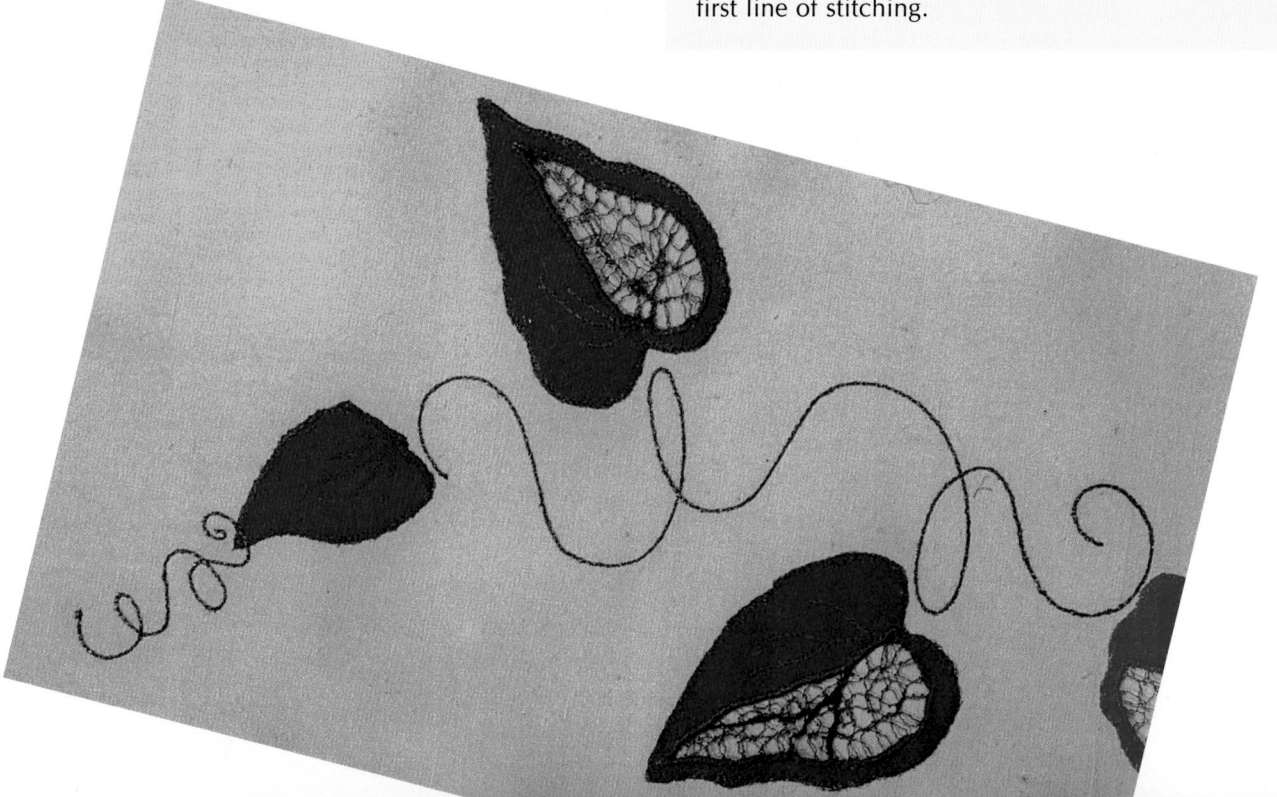

Appendix

SAMPLE PATTERNS

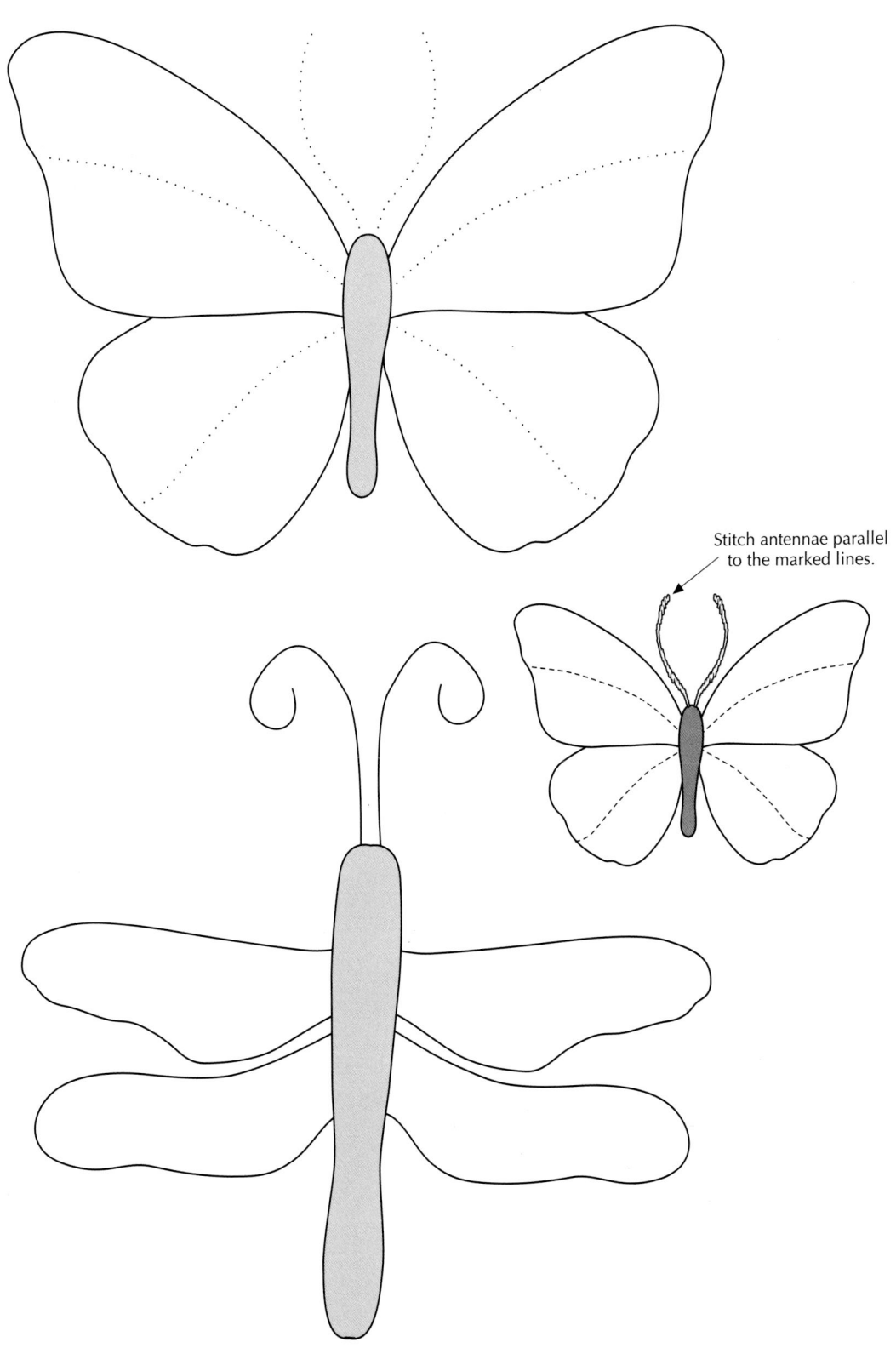

Stitch antennae parallel
to the marked lines.

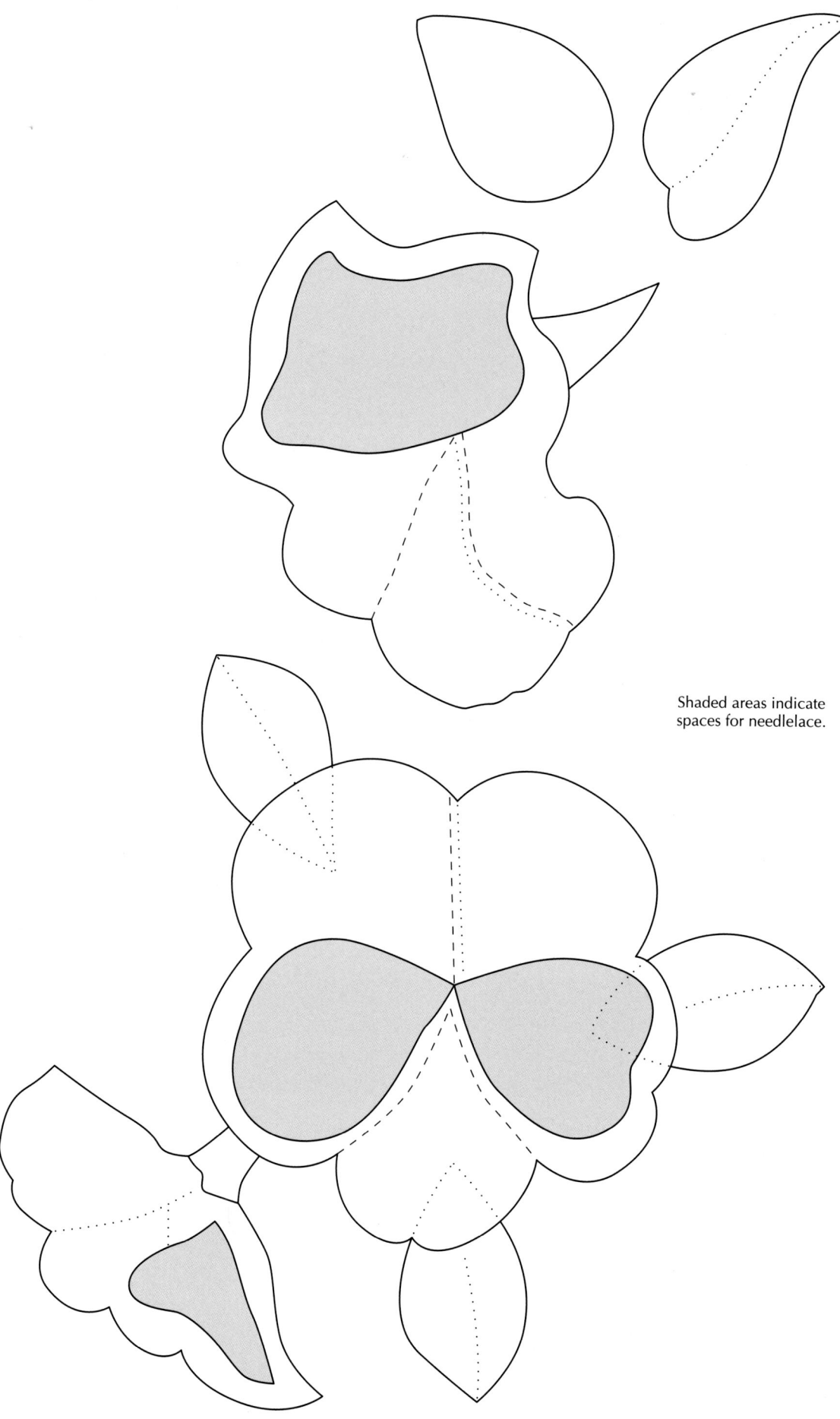

Shaded areas indicate
spaces for needlelace.

Shaded areas indicate
spaces for needlelace.

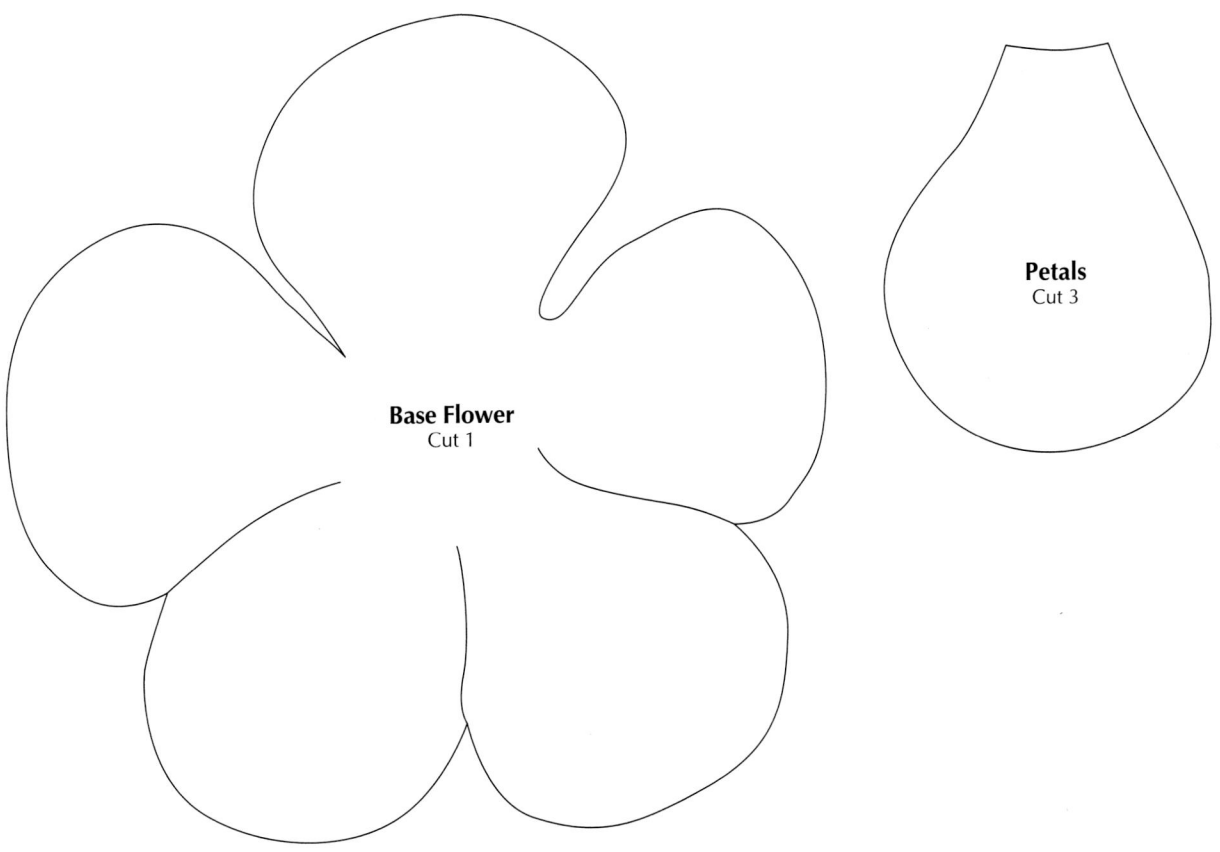

Base Flower
Cut 1

Petals
Cut 3

Resources

Dover Publications, Inc.
31 East Second Street
Mineola, NY 11501
Copyright-free design books

Web of Thread
1410 Broadway
Paducah, KY 42003
Specialty threads, stabilizers, hoops

Dharma Trading Co.
PO Box 150916
San Rafael, CA 94915
Deka silk paints and silk-painting supplies

Thai Silk
252 State Street
Los Altos, CA 94022
*Beautiful silk fabrics in a variety
of weights and weaves*

Clotilde
1909 S.W. First Avenue
Fort Lauderdale, FL 33315-2100
Large variety of sewing supplies

Nancy's Notions
333 Beichl Avenue
Po Box 683
Beaver Dam, WI 53916-0683
Large variety of sewing supplies and notions

About the Author

Judy Simmons grew up in New York, surrounded by talented and high-spirited women who believed nothing was impossible. She lived next door to her grandmother who, along with her mother, considered sewing a necessary component to one's well being. Judy grew up believing that sewing was as much a part of one's daily routine as sleeping and eating. Her early passion for sewing turned into a career when she earned her degree in home economics from Oneonta State University in New York. Judy taught junior high school for many years before venturing out on her own. She loved teaching and wanted to make a memory quilt, using all the leftover scraps from her students' projects. She took a few quilting lessons and was hooked.

Judy continues to make quilts, but especially enjoys making clothing because of the extra dimension associated with creating garments. She especially likes using a wide variety of fabrics—even some not normally used for clothing. To supplement her fabric stash, Judy has developed many of her own methods for enhancing natural-colored fabric with marbling, painting, dyeing, batiking, and airbrushing. She loves decorative threads and yarns and enjoys using them to embellish her work.

Judy's award-winning quilts and wearables have been exhibited throughout the country. Her exquisite clothing designs have appeared on the runway nationally and internationally in the prestigious Fairfield Fashion Show. In addition, her work has been published in *Quilter's Newsletter Magazine, Quilt, American Quilter, Sewing and Fine Needlework, McCall's Quilting, Craft and Needlework Age, Lady's Circle Patchwork Quilts,* and *Quilt World.*

Judy has taught and lectured throughout the United States as well as in Canada and Japan. Her classes are varied, covering all areas of creative machine techniques, fabric painting, and marbling.

For class and lecture information, contact:
Judy Simmons
3387 Bridle Run Trail
Marietta, GA 30064